T0150221

Cripple Joe
STORIES FROM MY DADDY

ALSO BY DONALD DAVIS

Tales from a Free-Range Childhood

Listening for the Crack of Dawn

See Rock City

Southern Jack Tales

Jack and the Animals

Ride the Butterflies

Barking at a Fox-Fur Coat

Mama Learns to Drive

Don't Kill Santa: Christmas Stories

The Pig Who Went Home on Sunday

Thirteen Miles from Suncrest: A Novel

Telling Your Own Stories

Writing As a Second Language

JOHN F. BLAIR, PUBLISHER
Winston-Salem, North Carolina

Cripple Joe
STORIES FROM MY DADDY

DONALD DAVIS

JOHN F. BLAIR,
PUBLISHER
1406 Plaza Drive
Winston-Salem, North Carolina 27103
www.blairpub.com

PRINTED IN CANADA

Library of Congress Cataloging-in-Publication Control Number: 2016012214 (print)

ISBN 978-0-89587-667-6
ISBN 978-0-89587-668-3 (ebook)

10 9 8 7 6 5 4 3 2 1

DESIGN BY DEBRA LONG HAMPTON
COVER IMAGE COURTESY OF DONALD DAVIS

For my cousin Ruth, with admiration and love

Contents

Author's Note

Our family stories are the identity carriers of our lives. We know who we are only if we know the stories of those people from whom we have come and the places they occupied in their lives.

Sometimes, we have a few photographs that have survived, but do we also have the stories that go with them? A picture may be worth a thousand words, but what if we are missing those thousand words? What if all we can do is look at the photograph and wonder, *What is that about?*

This is a picture book made of words. Some of the pictures are small, and some are large. Some are pictures of my father, some are pictures that he took, some are pictures in which he only stands on the side. All of the words in these stories are attempts to flesh out "the picture behind the picture," otherwise known as "the story."

My hope is that, as readers explore the pictures of my stories, they will find parallels to their own memories. If they do, then their stories will begin to become important to them, and perhaps they, too, will seek out the words behind the pictures—and even find themselves invisibly hiding there.

A Second Chance

My father, Joseph Simmons Davis, was born in 1901, the eighth of my grandfather's thirteen children.

There were two families on my father's side.

My grandfather Joseph Smawley Davis was born in Iron Duff, a township in the north end of what is now Haywood County in the western mountains of North Carolina, on December 9, 1852. When he was twenty-six years old, he married Nancy Jane Medford. She was sixteen years old. In the eleven years of their marriage, five children were born. Three of them died, the story goes, of whooping cough between ages three and six. Then Nancy Jane died at age twenty-seven. When I asked my father whether she, too, died of whooping cough, he replied, "It may have just been old age"—the old age of bearing five children and burying three of them by the time she was twenty-seven.

Grandfather took the two surviving children, Grover and Flora, and returned to live with his own parents until these children were themselves mostly grown. He then, in 1895, married my grandmother Ella Moody, who at twenty-seven was the same age Nancy Jane had been when she died. She and my grandfather then had eight additional children, the last of whom was born when he was fifty-nine and she was forty-two.

In my childhood, everyone in Daddy's family seemed to be old. My uncle Grover, his half-brother, born New Year's Day in 1885 (between the election and inauguration of Grover Cleveland as president), was the oldest relative I knew in childhood. My father was forty-three when I was born. The whole bunch seemed to a child like they had been here forever, and that they would live likewise.

The first four children born of the second marriage were boys. They seemed to me to have come into the world together, and they were inseparable of heart even through adulthood. There was Uncle Moody, the oldest, then Uncle Harry, then my father. My father's name, Joe, was somewhat unusual, in that he was the eighth-born child in the family and the fifth-born son, yet he was the one who was finally given his own father's name. The last of those four boys was Daddy's little brother, Uncle Frank.

In childhood, they did everything together. In fact, when they were quite small, a traveling photographer came through Iron Duff. In addition to family portraits, these four boys posed for a special photograph. Uncle Frank, barely old enough to walk, and my daddy were in little chairs in front. Harry and Moody stood in the back. Frank was holding a little stick in his hand in the photo. From then on, every few years, they would gather and have another photograph taken with the four of them posed in the same positions. Gradually, the little stick from childhood changed into a walking cane in the pictures.

I loved these three uncles. They were all like magicians to me, and when they came to visit or when we visited them, I wanted the time to last forever.

Uncle Harry lived with Aunt Zula and our cousins Margaret and Ruth in the little town of Leaksville, a long drive from where we lived. Uncle Harry was an automobile dealer.

At birth, he was named Faraday. It seems that my grandfather, who was in the North Carolina legislature at the time, had a great

Clockwise from top left are Uncle Moody, Uncle Harry, Uncle Frank, and Daddy as I best remember them. Taken in 1949, when I was about five years old.

close friend in the legislature by the name of Mr. Faraday. Some in the family even thought that Mr. Faraday and Grandfather were sometime-roommates sharing a hotel room in Raleigh when they were there for the winter legislative session. So the baby carried forth Mr. Faraday's name. It was a difficult name for others to understand and pronounce and promised to trouble the child his entire life.

The following year, Granddaddy went off to the legislature as usual. Went he got back home, he walked in the door of the house, pointed to baby Faraday playing on the floor, and pronounced, "We will call him Harry."

It was sometime later that the family learned that when Granddaddy had gotten back down to Raleigh for the legislative session, he learned that Mr. Faraday had turned Republican! That was more than he could abide, and so Faraday became Harry, and carried that name with him for the rest of his life.

At some time in his past, Uncle Harry had the tip of his forefinger cut off in some accident. Now, it was blunt and had a tiny fingernail that looked like a grain of popcorn. Every time we visited, he would show me his finger and ask me if I wanted to know what happened to it. I always fell for the bait.

Then he would tell me the sad story, except that every single time it was a different story of how he had come to lose the end of the finger. I loved these stories! In one story, a game rooster pecked his finger off, once it was cut off in the fan belt of a car, once slammed off when a window fell shut in his childhood, once bitten off by a shark in the Gulf of Mexico, another time blown off when his gun exploded. There was no end. If he had lost a thousand fingers, they might all have exited in a different way.

Children on their way to school passed in front of the car dealership, and Uncle Harry loved to visit with them. As a special project, he built a sort of robot-looking creature complete with yellow light-bulb eyes. The body was made of a metal trash can, legs and feet from lengths of stovepipe, arms of more stovepipe, head of a galvanized bucket. The robot's mouth was an old radio speaker.

The metal character was on small wheels so that, tethered by a slender wire cable, it could be slowly let down the sloping drive from the car dealership to the driveway and the sidewalk. The speaker-mouth was connected by wire to a microphone inside the building, where Uncle Harry could watch out the window and talk through the robot.

The children would come up to it, and he, watching hidden inside the building, would call them by name and talk with them. It was so fascinating that finally the little robot would have to be pulled back up the slope so the children could continue on home from school.

Uncle Moody lived with Aunt Rebekah in the nearby little town of Spray. They had no children. But Uncle Moody also loved children. Their house was in a new development where there were lots of neighbor children for him to entertain and play with.

As he gradually discovered, most of these children had grown up in town and had little acquaintance with country life. It seemed to be his role to educate them in rural ways, so that they would know things that they needed to know about the realities of the world.

So, one day as he traveled home from work at the wholesale grocery company, he stopped by the farm supply store and bought two bales of straw. After that, he stopped by the grocery store and got two quart bottles of milk.

Once home, he took the bales of straw back into the edge of the woods behind the house, took them apart, and built a large nest about six feet across on the ground. He put the two glass bottles of milk in the middle of the nest.

That afternoon, as the children came by on their way home from school, he called to them, "Come with me, kids. Come back here behind the house and see what I found in the woods. It's a cow's nest!"

The children, who had never seen a cow's nest, quickly followed. There in the woods, they saw it—a big straw nest on the ground, exactly the size for a sleeping cow. And it was complete with the two glass bottles of milk she had "laid" in the night. The kids eagerly ran home to tell their parents of the great discovery in Mr. Davis's woods!

Every afternoon, they would stop by to see how much milk the cow had laid, secretly hoping to catch the cow on her nest. They never caught the cow, but one afternoon they discovered that the cow had laid two quarts of chocolate milk!

"How did she do that?" one little girl cried.

Great discussion followed until a clever little boy solved it: "She lays chocolate milk in the dark!"

Uncle Moody also cultivated a chewing-gum tree in the front yard. Though it looked a lot like a black locust, when it "bloomed" in the springtime, the tree was covered with unwrapped sticks of various flavors of chewing gum. All the children had to do on the way home from school was pull the gum out from where it emerged from cracks in the bark, and it was ready to chew.

The third of these brothers, Uncle Frank, I saw much more often. It was he who now lived on the farm where Daddy was born and grew up, and we often went there on weekends to visit. Uncle Frank was the fearless childhood daredevil and inventor of problematic ideas—a habit that did not end when he grew up.

My father, Joe, was as interesting to me as any of the uncles. He worked at First National Bank in Waynesville, and whenever my mama wanted to go somewhere without me, she would drop me off at the bank in the afternoon to stay with Daddy.

In those days, the banks were open from nine until one— "banker's hours." This was because there was no separate bookkeeping department at the bank. At one o'clock, the bank closed and the tellers became the bookkeepers. They each entered their work from the morning and carefully checked everything until all the columns balanced. Sometimes they were finished before five, and sometimes they had to go back after supper and work until everything on the books was perfect.

So, anytime it was after one o'clock, my mother knew that she was free to leave me at the bank without interfering with customers. I loved it. The tellers were young women who had no children, and I was their toy. They spoiled me and bought me toys and treats.

They also let me play with the machines at the bank. They would assign me to a big hand-cranked adding machine that produced a paper-tape record of whatever you did, and then tell me to add up all the numbers in the Waynesville telephone directory. By the end of the afternoon, I would have paper tape all over the floor, though I never completed the addition assignment.

My daddy also let me play with the coin separator. It was a set of stacked trays with holes of diminishing sizes in each lower tray. You would dump a load of mixed coins on top, then shake the trays back and forth. In a few minutes, each tray contained its own set of coins—half-dollars on the top and dimes on the bottom. I could do that over and over again and never get tired of it.

Sometimes, Mama would leave me at the bank with Daddy even during the hours when the bank was open and customers were coming in and out. On occasion, some adult would come into the bank with a child I knew from school—sometimes a friend, often just an acquaintance. When that happened, I would tell Daddy, "I know that one!"

He would reply, "Then let's do it!"

I would go up to the kid I knew from school and talk a little bit. Then I would offer, "My daddy works here at the bank, you know. Do you want him to show you where they keep the money? He might show you, since you're such a good friend of mine."

Of course, the kid would agree. Daddy would give a wink to the parent, who waited patiently for this educational moment. We would take the little kid back through the door of the huge Mosler vault, past the rows of safe-deposit boxes, and on to the back, where there were bars separating us from the rear portion of the vault. Daddy would point through the bars at canvas bags he told us were filled with coins and flat canvas cases for currency.

Then, while the little kid was mesmerized with fascination, Daddy and I would slip out of the vault, quietly close the big door, and turn out the vault light. Then we would stand there and wait for a minute or two while the little kid screamed his head off inside the dark vault.

After an appropriate interval, Daddy would open the door back up and let the kid out. Then came his spoken warning: "That's what we do to every robber who ever comes into this bank. So you better not be one!"

There never was a bank robbery in Waynesville. My daddy scared it out of every child who grew up there. And the parents were appreciative, in that he saved them the reputation of parents who raised a child who turned out to be a bank robber!

All through my growing-up life, I was surrounded by these four men and their antics.

It was in the summer after my tenth grade in high school, and my parents had come to pick me up at the end of a week of band camp at Western Carolina Teachers College. As soon as I got into the car, Mama told me, "Your uncle Harry died yesterday. He had a heart attack. As soon as we get home, you need to pack your clothes so we can go on to Leaksville for the funeral."

I was shocked.

This was the first family funeral I remember attending. We indeed packed our clothes and left the following day. It was a five-hour drive to Leaksville, a long and tiring trip for a family that had no travel habit.

"We're not going to stay at their house. Zula doesn't need company on top of this," Mama told us. Staying in a motel was a totally new adventure for us as a family.

We arrived, got dressed, and went to the funeral home. We were going, as Daddy told us, "to see the corpse that Harry made." It was my second dead body to see, the first being Jody Palmer, a neighbor of my other grandparents, who had drowned when he was five years old. While I knew the Palmers as a family, I did not personally know Jody. So Uncle Harry was the first dead person I knew.

When we got there, I do not know what I expected. I guess I thought he would "look dead," whatever that meant. No, he simply looked asleep and healthy, though dressed up as for church. What seemed strange to a puzzled fifteen-year-old was that, as good as he looked, they would close the casket and bury him like that. It was a confusing age for a boy unexposed to the major issues of life.

What I remember most strongly is this: Daddy, Uncle Frank, and Uncle Moody walked into the church together and sat on the front row with Aunt Zula and my cousins Margaret and Ruth. Mama, brother Joe, and I sat on the pew behind them. It was then, when I saw the three brothers sitting together but, without even thinking, leaving a space for the missing fourth, that Uncle Harry's death had its strongest impact. It was not a single individual who had died, but one-fourth of a corporate entity of brothers who had been always as one. A part of each of them and, by extension, a part of me was now gone. He was sixty-one years old.

Eight years later, I was married and in graduate school when my mother called. I could hear the pain in her voice before the content of her message came over the line. Her call was to tell me that she had gone to a church women's meeting the night before. When she came home and walked in the door of the house, the look on my father's face was unlike any look she had ever seen before. She was sure that either my brother, Joe, or I had been killed in an accident.

"No," my father replied to her question, "it's my brother Moody. He had a heart attack and died this afternoon. He was doing some work inspecting houses for a realtor. When he went out to work and didn't come back, they went out to look for him. They found him dead in the empty house he had been sent to do the inspection on."

Two days later, I found myself again sitting on the second row, in a different church in Leaksville. On the row in front of me sat my father and his younger brother, Frank. They sat on either side of Moody's widow, Rebekah, as we all said goodbye to the second of those four brothers. Now, more of all of us was gone. He was sixty-nine years old.

Four years later, I had finished school and was living in

Lexington, North Carolina. My wife and I were only weeks away from the birth of our first child when my mother called again.

"It's your uncle Frank," she started. She could have stopped there, as I clearly knew what was coming next. "He went out to the barn to milk and didn't come back. Kathleen found him there. She called the ambulance, and they took him to the hospital, but Dr. Hammett told your daddy that Frank was dead way before they got him there. He probably died when he had the heart attack right there in the barn."

The funeral was on a Sunday afternoon. This time, I watched my father sit all alone with my aunt Kathleen and her children, Philip and Frances, as we said our goodbyes to his younger brother. Frank had just turned sixty-nine years old. A lot of the "us" was missing as I watched my father, now, of those four boys, all alone.

It was an early-April morning just a year later when I was awakened by the ringing of the telephone. At that time, I was a United Methodist parish minister and was not totally unaccustomed to phone calls coming in at odd and emergency hours. I reached out of bed and picked up the phone.

"Donald," the voice on the other end of the line said, and I already knew who was calling. It was the unmistakable voice of my cousin Kay. Kay and I were only a year apart in age. We had grown up together since we were born. I did not need to have her identify herself to know her voice. No, I knew who she was as she spoke my name.

Kay was the daughter of my mother's next younger sister, my aunt Eddie. They lived very close to us, were very close as sisters. In fact, as a sort of joke, Kay had always called both her mother and my mother "Mama."

"It's your daddy," she went on. "Mama just couldn't get him awake this morning. He is gone."

If you can be shocked but not surprised by news, that was the feeling that flowed into me. After his three brothers' sudden deaths, this certainly did not come around the corner of disbelief.

"Where's my mama now?" I asked.

"She's at the hospital. She called the ambulance, and they took him there anyway. I came back to call you, and her neighbor is going to bring her back when she's ready to leave him."

I was making plans in my head as clearly as I could. "We will get ready as soon as we can and be there as soon as we can get there. I need to wait until I can call some people before we can leave." We said goodbye.

It was a Thursday morning, and Sunday was coming. I knew that I would be out of church on Sunday and that plans for my absence needed to be made. When I looked at the clock, it was just past six-thirty—too early for phone calls. We would have to get ourselves ready and then wait a bit.

Suddenly, I was hit with an overwhelming feeling of panic. I was just beginning to realize that there was a lot about my father's life that I did not know. I was just beginning to enjoy asking him questions and hearing the stories of his childhood and early life before he met my mother, when he was already forty-two years old. Now, that was all over.

A million questions about him began to line themselves up in my mind. Where did he go to high school? I did not know! Did he get any education beyond that? What were his early jobs, and where did he live then? How did he meet my mother, and why did he not get married until he was in his forties? The questions went on and on. And now, they would forever be unanswered. He was suddenly gone.

I heard Douglas, our year-old first child, make a noise in his room. As I went in to lift him from his baby bed, emotion hit me again. This child would never know his grandfather.

The following three hours were miserable and mournful. When the call had come, it was too early in the morning for me to make phone calls for the plans to be away for a few days. I would have to wait until at least seven-thirty or eight o'clock to call some of the people who would need to fill in in various ways while I was gone for the funeral and whatever other things would need to be done before I could leave my mother alone and return to my normal life. It was a painful time of packing and waiting.

The waiting became haunting. I could not stop my mind from generating the questions. I knew little about my father's childhood except for overhearing the stories he and his brothers and sisters constantly retold each other when they were reliving the past. I knew nothing about his young-adult life before he met and married my mother. There were some sketchy outlines about where he worked, but I knew nothing at all of his individual and personal life. I was now only twenty-eight, my father was dead, and I had been too young and immature to know to ask for the stories that would have filled out his life for me.

Finally, all the calls were made and we were ready to go.

When I looked at the time, I realized that had we left soon after the call had come, we would be there by now. So I decided that the fair thing to do was to call my parents' house and let whoever was there know that we were just leaving Lexington and it would be another three hours before we arrived.

I hated making this call. My mother was never comfortable using the telephone, having grown up before there was a telephone in the house and always regarding it as an instrument of emergency. So it was almost always my father who answered the telephone whenever I called home through the years. Here was the pattern: I could call, their telephone would ring twice, then, predictably, my father would pick up the receiver, and I would hear, in his loud, cheerful voice, "Hello! This is Joe Davis. What can I do for you today?"

If the phone rang more than twice, I knew Daddy was not there and it would be my mother who was forced to pick up the telephone. There would be a good five or six rings, then I would hear the phone lifted, and, slowly, her quiet voice would enter a simple, "Hello."

"Hi, Mama!" I would reply.

"What's wrong?" was her predictable answer.

"Nothing's wrong!"

"Are you sick?"

"No, Mama, I was just calling you to see—"

She would break in, "Are the boys sick?"

"No one is sick. I was just thinking—"

"Do you need some money?" My mother was at her happiest when something was wrong. It was simply the way her mind was built.

On this day, I realized that my daddy would never answer the telephone again. It would be Mama. And in line with her telephone expectations, something on this day was indeed very, very wrong.

Slowly, I dialed the number—the same number we had had since it began with "Glendale-6" instead of "4-5-6." I waited for her familiar voice.

The telephone rang twice, then, suddenly, there it was. I heard someone pick up the phone and the clear voice: "Hello! This is Joe Davis. What can I do for you today?"

I dropped the phone. There was no answering machine playing a recorded message. No, it was my father himself, answering the telephone. As quickly as possible, I gathered up the dropped receiver from the floor and stupidly said, "You're supposed to be dead!"

Our conversation was not long. He was indeed alive.

We quickly got into our car to make the trip, now not to a funeral but to see him alive and to try to figure out what in the world had happened to create this strange and still-unbelievable scenario. All the way driving the three-hour trip, we were filled with a plethora of unanswered questions. It was before the day of cell phones, so we simply had to make the whole trip before we could begin to unravel the mysteries.

When we pulled up the hill of the driveway, Daddy met us at the car. He was in reality looking much more healthy than I felt at the moment. We hugged and spoke and headed into the house, where he and Mama were anxious to hear the whole story.

As my story of the phone call came out, there were no answers, only more questions. Mama and Daddy had no idea what I was talking about. Not only was my father not dead, everyone in even the extended family seemed whole and healthy.

We called my cousin Kay. Without telling her the details of what had happened, I simply asked whether she had called me earlier that day. No, she had made no phone call to me at all about anything, least of all to report a death that had never happened. No one could make any sense of it at all. The "sense" to me was, however, clear: my father had been experientially "dead" for about five hours and was—now, to me—totally alive and healthy again.

After a lovely weekend visit, we headed back home to Lexington, where the entire chain of events gradually became clear over the following days.

About a week or so before these events, a young man had moved from Lexington, Kentucky, to Lexington, North Carolina, to take a job as a reporter for the local newspaper, the *Lexington Dispatch*. I had noticed his Donald Davis byline several times in previous days and had even taken some kidding about whether I might be supplementing my income with a second occupation.

Well, it seemed that this Donald Davis also had a father whose name was Joe. His father—the Lexington, Kentucky, Joe Davis— had indeed died in the night, and it was his sister's duty to call him and give him the sad news.

In those 1970s days, the call had to be made on the normal landline. And since her brother, Donald Davis, had just moved, she did not have his new telephone number, if indeed he had managed to have a new phone installed in this short time. So she called "Information," and when she asked for a number for Donald Davis, she was given our number. It was a relief to her to believe that her brother did indeed have a phone and that she did indeed have his number.

From this point of discovery on, things gradually began to make more and more sense as the pieces came together. She had made the call believing she was calling her brother, Donald. Of course, she did not need to introduce herself. As brother and sister, they surely knew one another by the first word spoken. She did indeed hear my hello as belonging to her brother as surely and assumedly as I heard her first words as coming from my cousin Kay. Neither of us questioned the identity of the person on the other end of the line, nor did we ever question the content of the message. It made total sense to both of us all the way around.

So that was the story. The call was real. The identities were wrong but had so much of the ring of truth that the story played itself out with neither side raising a question.

Well, Daddy recovered from his first death and was in his ninety-third year when he died the next time. We had nearly twenty-two more years of him, and he got to see the birth of three grandsons and follow their paths almost all the way through the last one's being graduated from high school.

Here is what changed for me that day: I began asking questions, and my father began to tell me stories about his life. When we were visiting, he might, out of the blue, say, "Pick a year." I knew that he meant a year from his lifetime. I would randomly choose a year, maybe 1928, the year when he was twenty-seven years old, and he would begin, "Al Smith was running for president, and he was a Catholic, and Daddy said he didn't know what to do because he had never voted for either a Catholic or a Republican. . . ." And a whole story would come pouring out as he began to remember. The more he told, the more he remembered.

The real truth is that, up to the experience of his first "death," everything in even this story is something I learned after he came back to life on that April day. Almost all of the stories that I tell about him to this day did not even exist before the rebirthing following his first death. That happening blessed us with the finest relationship we could ever have had.

If you, in mourning the death of a beloved person, have ever said or even thought of what it would be worth to have them back with you for even a single day, think of this: start asking the questions and telling the stories now. You may not have my second chance.

The Swimming Hole

The first stories I remember hearing in childhood were my father's stories. They did not come easily. In fact, he denied ever telling stories. His claim was that his younger brother, my uncle Frank, was the only storyteller in the family. When Daddy did offer what he would have called "a story," it usually began with the words, "Frank used to tell about . . ."

Added to his reluctance was the reality that I paid very little attention to these stories when they did come. Early on, I came to believe that he had no stories worth listening to. It was only after his first "death" that I began to try to pull back the memories of stories from him.

Sometimes, I loved the remembered stories when he told them. Sometimes, I did not. Mostly, I loved them when I could make no personal connection between the story and my own immediate behavior. I did not at all love them when the story being told directly paralleled what I happened to be doing. I gradually realized that he was quite a genius at this.

The first story I remember is one of the few that was told

over and over again. It seemed to come out whenever my brother and I (or was I acting alone?) seemed to be undertaking a task with questionable possibilities of completion. Like most of these early stories, this one was of an event involving Daddy along with Moody, Harry, and Frank.

Daddy was number eight of thirteen children. Born in 1901, he was third in a cluster of four boys who came right in the middle of that long run of children. There was his brother Moody, born in 1897; his brother Harry, born in 1899; and his younger brother, Frank, born in 1903.

It was about 1910 and late summertime. The four boys, ages seven to thirteen, were working each day to help their father, my grandfather, do what they all called "making hay."

There were no motorized vehicles of any kind on the farm. In fact, the family was so far back in the mountains of North Carolina that a car had never made the trip to the house in Iron Duff. All of the machinery on the farm was powered by what Daddy always called "a team of big, blond Belgian workhorses."

They would first hook the mowing machine up to the workhorses. Then they would mow the hay. This was a complicated job in that the hayfields still had stumps scattered through them, since they had only recently been cleared as farmland from the forest. Harry would sit on the seat of the mowing machine and hold the reins of the horses. Daddy and Frank, being the younger ones, would take turns walking along at the end of the sickle-bar blade and watch for stumps. Moody, being the oldest, would walk beside the lead horse, holding it by the bridle so he could stop it immediately. When they came to a stump, the walker at the end of the blade would shout, "Stump!" and his brother would stop the horse. Then the end of the mowing blade would be lifted up so it could pass over the stump before being let back down to continue mowing. It was hard, slow, and dangerous.

After all the hay was mowed, the mowing machine was unhooked and the huge hay rake was hooked up. Usually, Granddaddy did the raking. He was never satisfied with the way the boys did

Daddy's family reunion about 1909, taken on the steps of his grandfather's home, still standing today in Haywood County. Photo includes my grandfather and his six brothers and one sister. Granddaddy is the one with the beard near the center. My grandmother, at his right shoulder, is holding baby Mary. Granddaddy is holding Lee and Esther. To his left, the boys go in ascending order: Frank, Daddy (smallest one), Harry, Moody, and (standing with an uncle's arm around him) half-brother Grover. Half-sister Flora, already married and with her own children, is on the back row near the center wearing a black bow tie.

it. Besides, there was plenty of work for everyone to stay occupied all the time.

The hay would be raked into long rows everyone called "wind rows." The mowing and first raking were usually spread out over a couple of days, and by now the hay was drying. Next, the wind rows were raked into small piles, just the right size to be loaded onto the wagon. Pulled by the horses, the wagonloads of hay would be taken back to the barn.

At the end of the barn were two tall poles. They were actually tall, skinny tree trunks that had been set into the ground at the east end of the barn. Here is where the hardest part of the work started. Two or three of the boys would climb up onto the wagon and fork the hay off the wagon at the base of one of the big poles. Granddaddy and the remaining boy would arrange the unloaded hay around and around the pole, shaping it just right so it would shed rainwater at the top, until they had at last built the two gigantic haystacks that would feed the cows all winter.

It was late August, and they spent over a week making hay. It was an exhausting job.

Worse than this, though, was that hay making was itchy. By the end of the day, all the brothers would have hay in their hair, hay down their backs, hay up their noses, hay in their eyes. They would be itching to death all over.

Though Granddaddy had built their new house, all clapboard on the outside, in 1903, it had no electricity and no running water. There was a good springhouse in the back and a two-seat outhouse up the hill. But there was no bathroom in the house and no provision for bathing other than filling a tin tub on the back porch. Bathing was difficult and seldom.

So, at the end of each hay-making day, the four brothers would head out for the Pigeon River. It was a good mile walk, but in the end it was worth it. They would strip off their hay-infested clothes and shake them out as hard as they could, trying to dislodge all of the itchy debris. Then they would jump, all naked, into the Pigeon River.

When, as a child, I heard Daddy tell about swimming in the Pigeon River, I did not believe the story. This was because, between his childhood days and mine, the Pigeon River had been totally poisoned and polluted by discharge from the Champion Paper and Fiber Company in Canton. Whenever we rode beside the river on the way to his childhood home, we had to hold our noses because of the sulfuric smell. The river looked like dark tea, with foamy and even solid waste floating on top of the blackened water. I could not believe that they had ever swum in that water!

In the years since then, however, the river has been remarkably cleaned up. You can once again see into the water, the odor is all gone, and fish have returned. It is even again possible to swim and play in the water as it was in his old story.

The four boys would swim around, splashing each other and playing in the cool water of the river. They would pick up handfuls of sand where it settled in the calm places at the edge of the water and use the sand to scrub all the itch off their bodies. The swimming and playing went on until all four knew that it was near time for supper. Then they came out of the water, ran around naked until they were dry, gave their clothes another good shaking, dressed, and went home, better ready now for a night of sleep without itching to death.

One afternoon when the haying work was done, the brothers started to troop to the river when little brother Frank had an idea. It wasn't at all unusual for Frank to be the one to get the idea because, Daddy often told us, in their family Frank was "in charge of bad ideas."

"It is too far," he spoke up, "for us to walk a mile every afternoon to jump into the river and get washed off. What we need is a swimming hole here at home."

"What's a swimming hole?" one of the brothers asked.

"I read about it in a book," Frank returned. "It's a big hole in the ground beside your house. It is filled with water, and anytime you take a notion you just go out there and jump in. I figure we ought to dig one!"

Daddy spoke up next. He always claimed to us to be the voice of reason in the family. "That sounds dangerous, Frank. I don't think that Mama and Daddy would let us do that."

"I already thought of that." He was ready. "That is why we are not going to tell them. Let's dig it over there on the back side of the big rock behind the house, so that if anyone looks out they will not see what we're doing. Then, when we get it dug and all filled up with water, we can show it to them, and they will like it so much they will want to jump in, too!"

Daddy looked at his three brothers. Harry and Moody looked like they were in complete agreement with Frank. Finally, he spoke up. "Well, boys, I will stay and watch while you get in trouble, but I am not going to do a thing to help."

The boys went out to the big barn in search of tools for digging the swimming hole. They came out dragging a short spade and a big shovel, a pickax, two garden hoes, and an old mattock. The tools were awkwardly carried around the house and to the back side of the big rock that stuck about six feet up out of the ground there. Frank scratched out a square pattern on the ground, and the work started.

It was August when all this was going on, and the late-summer ground was so hard and dry that a shovel would not begin to break the surface. They almost gave up when Harry got an idea. "I know what let's do. Let's take turns chopping the hard dirt loose with the mattock. When we get some loose, then let's shovel it out with the shovel, and then chop some more loose."

Daddy just shook his head. He could easily tell that with this plan they would have a finished swimming hole in about a hundred years. The work started.

Since the mattock was Harry's idea, he took the first turn. He chopped the wide blade hard into the dry soil and began to make slow progress in breaking up the hard surface. Frank and Moody watched, along with Daddy, for a few minutes until Frank became too impatient to keep standing there doing nothing. He picked up the big shovel and began to toss the loose dirt over to the side.

In addition to being in charge of bad ideas, there was another thing about Frank. In the family, it was said that Frank was born with a slight birth defect: he was born without a lid to go on his mouth! It ran wide open all of the time. Frank woke up talking in the morning, he talked through every meal with food in his mouth, and he fell asleep talking at night. As soon as he was asleep, he even talked in his sleep. Besides that, Daddy said, all the talking must have used Frank's entire mentality, because when he was talking he was not capable of doing anything else.

A picture began to emerge: Harry chopping with the mattock, Frank talking and digging at the same time, Harry coming back with the mattock, Frank bending over with the shovel, Harry coming down with the mattock and chopping Frank right in the crown of his head.

Blood squirted everywhere, and Frank began to squall, "I am kilt! I am kilt! I am kilt!"

Harry took him on immediately. "You are not killed or you could not holler like that!"

All four boys went running toward the house.

As I listened to Daddy tell the story, I could imagine my poor grandmother calmly washing dishes in the kitchen until she heard terrible and confusing noises outside the house. When she opened the door, here came running her four boys. The one in front had blood almost squirting out of his head. Behind him came another one carrying a shovel and another one carrying a mattock. They all came running into the house.

My grandmother grabbed her dishrag and washed it out in cold water. Then she held it firmly against the top of Frank's head. It was quickly soaked in blood. She washed it out again in the cold water and put on more pressure. After several minutes of this, the blood finally stopped, and she looked to examine his wounded head.

"So that's what the bone looks like!" was all she said.

In addition to the wound itself, there was another major problem: the farm was sixteen miles from town on an unimproved dirt road. The only way to get to town was to walk or ride a horse. Besides that, they never went to town. Everything they ate, everything they wore, they made themselves right there on the farm. And they did not even know a doctor.

My grandmother quickly concluded that she would have to work on Frank herself. She walked over to the kitchen sink and got my grandfather's straight razor from the shelf where it stayed above the sink. She opened the razor and stropped it on the razor strop until it was clean and sharp. Then she had Frank kneel down while she carefully shaved off all of the hair around the crown of his head where he was cut. While she was doing this, she had dropped something into a pan of water she set to boil on the wood stove.

When the shaving was done, she called on Moody, Harry, and

Daddy to come over and help hold Frank so he couldn't run away. While they held him, she fished into the boiling water and pulled out a needle and thread she had put there. And while the three boys held their brother, their mother sewed up his head!

Their father, my grandfather, had come in from the barn while all this was going on. He did not volunteer to help, but simply watched it all with interested amazement. Then he said to my grandmother, "Ella, how did you know how to do that?"

"I didn't know," she offered. "I just figured it out myself. I've read about people getting sewed up, and I figured that was the only way to close up a cut like that. I don't know if I did it right. I reckon you had better take him to town and see if you can find a doctor and see if I got it right. It might have to be done over again."

So, now that Frank was all sewed up, Grandfather got one of the workhorses from the barn. He got up on the horse and got Frank up in front of him. They headed for town. It was after dark by the time they got there.

Daddy's older half-brother, Grover, was already grown up and married and lived in town. They went to Grover's house and spent the night there. The next morning, Grover helped them find the doctor's house, and Grandfather took Frank to get his head checked out.

The doctor closely and carefully examined Frank's head. He felt of it and poked and prodded. Finally, he looked content with the examination and asked my grandfather three questions.

"Did this boy's own mother actually sew up his head?"

"Yes, she did."

"Did she boil the needle and thread before she sewed with them?"

"She did indeed." (I do not know how she knew to do that.)

There was one last question: "Does she make quilts?"

"Yes," Grandfather answered. "How come you ask?"

"Well," the old doctor smiled, "if I had sewed up a cut like this, I would likely have put in about six stitches. As well as I can count, she has given him thirty!"

Grandmother had stitched Frank up with tiny stitches just like the ones she used in making quilts that would last over a hundred years.

The doctor went on. "She has done such a neat little job that it might not even leave a scar when it heals up. If she ever wants a job, tell her to come to see me!"

Then the doctor pulled out a big brown glass bottle that was filled with something called iodine. He took a cotton swab and painted the iodine all over the shaved part of Frank's head. Frank started squalling, "I'm kilt again! I'm kilt again!" as the iodine was burning his head terribly. Soon, though, things settled down, and he and my grandfather rode the big horse home.

Once back at home, Frank was the star of the show. Everyone looked at his head and heard the story over and over again of what a good job their own mother had done in sewing up their brother's head. Finally, Frank himself got two mirrors situated so he could see the top of his own head. He was amazed. There, he saw that he had a whole swath of his hair shaved off. Then he could see the stripe where he was sewed up by his mama. And on top of that, he was painted all reddish brown with the iodine.

He must have happily thought to himself, *I am so funny looking! They will never make me go to church looking like this!* But they did. Grandfather later said that there had not been that much laughter at the Methodist church for twenty-five years. Frank had to answer questions from almost every single person who was there.

On Sunday afternoon after dinner, when the whole family was settled down, Grandfather gathered the four boys together for a little talk. "Well, boys, I guess you know by now that you should not have done this. You all know that there ought to be some kind of punishment for a thing like this. But you know what I always say—if you learn something from what you do, that is better than punishment. So, if each one of you can tell me about something you learned from all of this, there will not have to be any punishment. Moody, you are the oldest, so you go first. Did you learn anything from all this business?"

Moody thought for only a brief moment before he answered. "Yes, sir, I did. We do not need a swimming hole!"

Grandfather smiled. "That is good enough! Now, Harry, did you happen to learn anything?"

It took Harry a little longer. No one knew whether he was trying to think of something or whether he was trying to decide on actually saying what he had already been thinking all the time. "Yes, sir, I did learn something for sure. If you ever have to get a whole lot of blood out of somebody, you need to hit them right square in the top of the head!"

Grandfather chuckled. "I guess you are actually right about that, Harry. That will do for you. Now, Frank, did you yourself happen to learn anything?"

Frank took no time at all to think. It was obvious that he had figured things out long before the question was even asked. "I sure did! This is it: if two people are working, and one of them has a shovel and one of them has a mattock, you had better be the one who has the mattock! I know that for sure."

Grandfather laughed out loud this time. "That's good, Frank. That is surely good! Now, Joe, did you happen to learn anything, even if you were just watching what was going on? I know that you are a good observer."

Daddy was about nine years old when all of this happened. Each time he told us about it, it seemed that he was back to being nine years old again.

He carefully framed his answer. "I did learn from watching, and this is what I think about the whole thing. If I ever grow up and have children of my own, I am going to tell them that their uncle Frank is the best teacher that they will ever have. I am going to tell them to ask him questions, ask him questions, ask him questions—and then do not do a single thing that he says!" He went on. "Actually, I had already learned that before this happened, but all this swimming-hole business just showed me that I was right about Frank again."

And in our own childhood, my brother, Joe, and I did just what he suggested.

Uncle Frank and the Skunk

Many of the stories I remember Daddy telling involved Uncle Frank's bad ideas. Sometimes, what he seemed to think was a bad idea I thought to be both funny and wonderful. Even when I was still a small boy, Uncle Frank was one of the favorite family characters in my life. I loved going to his house (the farm where Daddy had grown up), and I loved it when he and Aunt Kathleen came to our house. There was always a story to be remembered from an Uncle Frank visit.

I well remember one Sunday afternoon when I was probably in junior high school. We were all at home when in the late afternoon we heard a car coming up the driveway. I looked out the window and saw Uncle Frank's old yellow Mercury. It was a good sign that this would be a more interesting day than it might have been. I headed to the door to welcome him in.

It was both Uncle Frank and Aunt Kathleen. They were all dressed up like they had just come from church, though it was quite late in the day. Besides being dressed up, Uncle Frank was laughing his head off. He just kept chuckling out loud and couldn't seem to stop.

Daddy came into the living room. "Frank and Kathleen! I thought that was your car."

Uncle Frank couldn't speak. He was now laughing out loud.

"What's so funny?" Daddy asked. "And why are you still dressed up for church so late in the day?"

Aunt Kathleen just shook her head. She was used to this by now and didn't want to give these goings-on her blessing.

"We've been to Guy Chambers's funeral." Then he let out with another big laugh.

"Poor old Guy. I didn't know he had died," Daddy replied. "But what is so funny about going to somebody's funeral?"

"It was so good. It was almost worth having Guy die just to get to go to the funeral."

At this, I knew something good was coming, and I wasn't about to miss a word of it.

Uncle Frank started to unfold the story. He reminded all of us about how he always liked to be the first person to get everywhere. On the day of the funeral, he had hurried Aunt Kathleen up after Sunday dinner so they could be the first ones there for the three o'clock funeral. They got to the church way ahead of time, but when they drove up into the parking lot another vehicle was already there. For a moment, he was discouraged because he thought someone had beaten him at being first. Then he realized that the vehicle was a panel truck from the funeral home. It had been driven by the gravedigger, who had opened the grave the day before and had come back early in the day to be sure that everything was in good shape for the funeral.

As soon as Uncle Frank's car came into the parking lot, the gravedigger came running. He was jumping up and down and waving his arms in the air and seemed to be very upset. "Help, help!" the gravedigger kept yelling. "Stop everything! Stop the funeral!"

Uncle Frank said he tried to calm the man down. "We can't stop the funeral," he said. "Guy is already dead. Now, what is the trouble?"

The family home, built in 1903 and new here, burned in 1949. Daddy is the baby held by his father. The others are my uncles.

Then the gravedigger explained everything. Yes, he had opened the grave the day before. Yes, he had come back early to be sure that everything was in order. Then, when he was checking everything out, he discovered that a big skunk had fallen into the open grave during the night. Now, there was a big, wild skunk six feet down in the ground where Guy was supposed to go.

Uncle Frank knew that they couldn't put Guy in the ground with the skunk, even though he knew that the two of them would get along just fine together. "Well, let's go have a look," he offered to the gravedigger, "and see what we can figure out."

The two men walked up from the church parking lot to the country cemetery. It was on a pretty hilltop surrounded by woods on the back side. I was told that when the cemetery was located there, my great-great-grandfather could stand on the top of this hill and know that he owned all the land that could be seen.

There, on the side of the graveyard, Uncle Frank could see the funeral-home tent and a pile of red clay beside the opened grave.

He and the gravedigger walked over and together looked down into the six-foot-deep hole in the ground.

Sure enough, there in the bottom of the grave, a big, fat skunk was making his nearsighted circuit around and around, just as if he assumed that on the next round he might find his way out. Guy was not going to be put down in this grave until, somehow, the skunk came out.

As Uncle Frank told us the story, I listened more intently than ever. I was pretty sure that it was about time for him to come up with one of his bad ideas. He did not hesitate as he went on to tell us what happened.

"I looked down at the skunk," he started. "Then I looked at the gravedigger. That's when it came to me!"

"Tell us!" I urged him on.

Uncle Frank had started in on the gravedigger. "Sir," he slowly began, "let's see if we can think our way out of this dilemma. We are smarter than that skunk, so we have the advantage. Now, answer this question for me: if that same skunk were standing right up here beside us on level ground, and he decided that he wanted to spray us, what is the last thing he would have to do before he could squirt?"

The man thought about it for a minute or so, then answered, "I reckon the last thing he would have to do is to lift up his tail."

"You are right." Uncle Frank was rolling now. "Now, think with me. We are on the verge of a solution. Look at that skunk. The way skunks are designed, that skunk has enough muscles in his tail to lift up his tail, sure enough. But if we should grab the skunk first and pick it up by the tail, it does not have enough muscles in its tail to lift the weight of its entire body, and we would have it locked shut!"

The man didn't seem to know whether to look pleased or puzzled.

Uncle Frank went on before the gravedigger could question his logic. "Now, sir, I would do this first part, but I hurt my knee and I just can't jump down in there. But if you will quickly jump down into the grave and grab the skunk by the tail, we will then have him locked up. I will stay right here waiting for the next step.

After you have locked him, hand him up here to me, and I will get him by the tail and carry him over to the fence. We will be on schedule, and no one will ever know that there was a problem."

"What happened next?" It was my brother, Joe, who had to ask the question.

"You don't smell anything, do you? We did it! He jumped down into the open grave and grabbed that skunk by the tail before the little animal even knew he was there. You should have seen that skunk. He was as mad as a wet hen. He was kicking all four legs and squealing, but he could not get into position to squirt. I knew that if he didn't squirt the gravedigger, then he could not squirt me. So I got him by the tail, carried him over to the back fence, and tossed him over into the woods. He ran as fast as he could to get way out of here. In no time, Guy was buried alone, and no one knew the difference."

It was Daddy's turn for a question now. "How did you know it would work, Frank?"

Uncle Frank smiled. "I didn't. That's the reason I talked him into jumping down in there to begin with. I was already figuring that if it didn't work, I didn't need to stay around any longer."

Later, at the end of the day, Daddy wanted to talk with Joe and me about what we had heard. "Now, boys," he started, sounding almost serious, "you know that I have always told you that your uncle Frank is the best teacher you will ever have. What did you learn today from what he told you?"

Joe seemed ready to go with his answer. "I learned something good. Since you never actually know how something is going to turn out, you might as well go ahead and try things whenever you take a notion!"

Daddy shook his head, but I could see him grinning as he looked at me. "Well, son," he said, reaching for my answer, "I hope you can do better than that."

"I can," I proudly announced. "If you don't know how something is going to turn out, you get somebody else to try it first!"

And thanks to Uncle Frank, that lesson has served me well ever since.

The Big Hunting Trip

In all of my growing-up memory, Daddy was not big on travel. We took only one real vacation in all of those years. It was a trip to Florida, all four days of which were spent in the car, two going and two coming back. I had no idea that in his younger days he had actually taken trips. I made this discovery when, in reading the letters he wrote to Mama before they were married, I found a series of postcards from a long trip to visit three brothers and sister Mary right in the middle of World War II.

After this discovery, I realized that one particular story, one that I had heard over and over again since childhood but paid no attention to, was actually more important than I ever thought. It was, among other formative things, the trip that probably established forever his distrust of travel as a positive activity.

It was 1929, and Daddy was twenty-eight years old. He was unmarried and boarding with a family called the Blaylocks. Daddy owned a house in Hazelwood, but he had discovered in his frugality that it was more lucrative for him to rent out the house he owned and then have a single room with the Blaylocks than to live all alone in his own house. He always saved his money.

For ten years or so, he had worked as the bookkeeper for the Blackwell and Bushnell Wholesale Grocery Company. Early on in this time, his father had died (in 1920) and he had taken on the role of surrogate father to his own five little brothers and sisters, who were now fatherless. He also took on the role of caring for his own mother and his unmarried aunt Laura, who was a member of the household. This job naturally fell to him, as all of the older brothers and sisters were already married and had lives of their own to take care of.

So Daddy's life was simple. He worked during the week, staying and eating with the Blaylocks and spending very little money on himself. On weekends, he went out to Iron Duff to see about his mother and Aunt Laura and take care of their needs.

He had recently changed jobs and gone to work as the accountant for a small manufacturing company called Royal and Pilkington (everyone called it "the rag mill"), which produced hand-woven upholstery materials. He still saved his money.

Two of Daddy's friends were called Rippetoe and Hawkins. One day, the three of them came up with a big idea. They had read about people going hunting for Canada geese along the coastline of North Carolina during the fall migratory season. Since they had enjoyed hunting together in the mountains of their youth, they decided they might go out to the eastern part of the state and try out a new brand of hunting.

It was not much of a plan, but in late October of that year the three of them took off from work for their big week-long adventure.

Daddy had the best car. It was a used Hudson touring car that he had bought from Mr. Blackwell, for whom he had worked at the wholesale grocery. They all agreed that the Hudson was the car to take on the trip.

Money would be needed to cover all of the costs. For his part, Daddy went to the bank and drew from his savings account. He had over a ten-year period of time saved up fifteen hundred and eighty-seven dollars. This amounted to a good percentage of his total earnings. As he thought about the trip, he had no idea what the costs might be. So he took out the eighty-seven dollars and left fifteen hundred in the bank.

Now, they were ready to go.

There was no actual North Carolina road map available for planning the trip. They had only a United States map and an idea about where they were going. They would ask for help along the way.

Daddy knew the way to get to Durham. His youngest brother, Lee, was going to college there at Duke University. Daddy had been the one to take him to school there, so he knew the way. Durham, North Carolina, was their goal for the first day.

They got the Hudson all packed the night before so they could get an early start. It was five in the morning when he left the Blaylocks' house and headed around to pick up Rippetoe and Hawkins. Once in the car, they headed toward Asheville.

Asheville was thirty miles, and it took them about an hour to get there. By then, they were all hungry, so they stopped at a restaurant just the other side of the Beaucatcher Mountain tunnel and had a big breakfast. They also talked over the way they were going. Daddy explained it all to them.

From Asheville, they went east through Black Mountain and on over the mountain road to Old Fort. Then they went on toward Marion and through there to Morganton. When they finally got to Hickory, it was time to stop for dinner and a little nap in the Hudson after they ate. "For digestion," Daddy told us as he repeated the story.

The drive from Hickory seemed endless. They were out of the mountains now, and the roads were almost too straight to be interesting. It was an endless drive from Hickory through the country to Mocksville, and then on through more endless country to Winston-Salem. From there to Durham, the drive was a little more interesting, as they went through a lot of little towns. The main sights were Kernersville, Greensboro, and Burlington.

At about five in the afternoon, they finally arrived in Durham. They checked in at the Jack Tar Hotel and then drove over to the campus to find Daddy's brother Lee. He was on the football team and lived in team quarters under the football stadium. Once they got with Lee, there was a big splurge as Daddy and his two hunting partners took him downtown to the Jack Tar and treated him to supper. When all the festivities of the visit were over, they returned Lee to his room and bedded down for the night. There were two beds in the Jack Tar Hotel room, and the three of them drew straws to see who got to sleep alone and which two had to share a bed. Daddy lost and had to sleep with Rippetoe.

They had planned to get an early start the next morning. But they discovered that the Jack Tar Hotel did not even begin to serve breakfast until six-thirty, so their early start was spoiled. The advantage, however, was that they could go around the dining room at breakfast and get advice about how to get to Lake Mattamuskeet, their goal for the day.

They were told to go first to Raleigh and then on to Kinston. Daddy really wanted to stop in Raleigh and see the Capitol building. His father, my grandfather, had been in both the North Carolina House of Representatives and the Senate. Daddy wanted to visit the building where his father had gone almost every winter of his remembered childhood. But with the late start, they simply drove past the Capitol as they went through town and out New Bern Avenue.

The advice was to go to Kinston and ask again there, so that was what they did. In Kinston, they were told to go to New Bern. By New Bern, they were starving, so they stopped at a restaurant beside the water and got fried fish. From New Bern, they were sent toward a place called Belhaven—and were also told by everyone they asked that they could have come a better way. No one, however, agreed on how they should have come.

By the time they got to Belhaven, they thought that surely they were almost where they were going. But there was more advice.

"You are almost there," said the pumper at the Standard Oil

station. "I can tell you exactly what to do. Stay on this road and go to Swan Quarter. When you get to Swan Quarter, ask around until you find the Campbells. They will put you up and feed you and make all of the arrangements for you boys to go hunting. Yes, ask for the Campbells."

It was late afternoon when the Hudson arrived in the town of Swan Quarter. The hardest thing was to find somebody to ask. When they finally decided to stop at a house and knock on the door, the very door on which they knocked actually turned out to be the Campbells'.

The Campbells told them that they took care of goose hunters all of the time and that they were in luck because the house was not full this year. They could have sleeping quarters, breakfast and dinner, and a packed lunch for the hunting for only five dollars a day. None of the three hunters had any idea that it would cost this much, but they agreed.

This was only the beginning. The Campbells informed them that this five dollars was only for room and board, and that for an additional five dollars each they would have their own guide, who would take them to a private duck blind, furnish them with all the ammunition they needed, and even supply live decoys to assure that they had a successful hunt. There was no going back now, so the agreement was made.

That night, they had a big meal of fried fish, collards, and hush puppies. Then they all fell asleep quickly after the two-day-long drive to get all the way across North Carolina. The pickup time was to be five in the morning, with breakfast before that at four-thirty.

It was still dark the next day when William, a black man with a mule and a wagon, picked the three great hunters up after the Campbells' big breakfast. They each had the shotguns that they had brought from home. Somehow, William already knew what the gauges were (all were 20-gauges) and had boxes of the right ammunition. They climbed onto the wagon and told the Campbells goodbye for the day.

There was hardly room to get up into the wagon, as it was

crowded with what looked like chicken crates. They were, however, filled with Canada geese, rather than with chickens. These were the mentioned live decoys. Each goose, they were soon to learn, had its wings clipped so it could not fly. They also each had small chains attached to rings on their legs. Daddy said he was anxious to see how all of this worked.

Their destination was the shore of Lake Mattamuskeet, just inland from the Pamlico Sound outside Swan Quarter. The trip seemed to go on forever. When they got to the planned location, it was just beginning to show daylight.

The duck blind was a fascinating structure to the three men. Daddy told us that you could walk right up on it and never see it unless you knew where it was. The blind had been made by digging a rectangular hole in the ground that was about eight by twelve feet in area and about four feet deep. On the water side of the hole, a log had been laid on the ground. Then, with notched supports on top of each end of this log holding it up about a foot, there was another log. The opening between the two logs was the support for the guns they were to shoot. From the top of the upper log, poles had been stretched back to roof the hole. The poles had then been covered with limbs and rushes and cattails, which had all dried together so that they looked like the ground all around. Even the opening to the blind was covered, and you had to lift up a mat of dried vegetation to enter.

William unloaded the chicken crates with the live decoys. He asked Daddy and Rippetoe and Hawkins if they would help carry the crates down to the edge of the water and also bring an armload of wooden stakes he had piled in the back of the wagon.

Once everything was in place, William began to take the live geese out of their crates. As he picked up each one, the small chain dangled from its leg. On the end of this chain was a clip that he fastened to a ring on one of the wooden stakes. William then waded out into the water until he was about knee deep. He put the goose down on the water and pushed the wooden stake deeply into the sandy bottom of the lake. Once set free, the geese didn't even act like they were going to try to get away. They just floated around and honked like they knew it was their job to draw in victims for the kill.

William led the mule with the wagon back into some bushes and out of sight. Then he returned to the blind and began to tell the men what the plan was. Pretty soon, William told them, the migrating geese would start to come over. When the live decoys began to honk, the geese flying over would think this might be a good place to land. When they came down, the men shouldn't shoot until the geese were right above the water. That's when they made the best targets, just as they slowed down to make a landing.

"Now," he said to the three men, "go to it!"

Daddy and the others did not now know exactly what to do. They had not seen any geese flying and were not sure if William was just leaving them on their own. But he settled back in the corner of the duck blind and proceeded to light a little kerosene heater they had not noticed before. The heater made the space almost cozy, but mostly it was the heat source for William as he fixed a pot of coffee to perk on its top. This was going to be a day of luxury!

In a little while, the live decoys began to stir around and get excited. In no time, they began to quack and honk. Daddy said that he looked out of the space between the logs and could see a big V of geese flying over Lake Mattamuskeet. They were heading right toward the duck blind. The decoys were honking to beat the band and thrashing around, though they could not take off. They seemed to be calling to the geese flying overhead.

The big V went into a large circle and came down toward the water. Daddy and Hawkins and Rippetoe got so excited they did not know what to do. "Wait for them, wait for them," was William's advice. The big geese looked like they were pedaling backwards with their wings as they came settling into the water with the live decoys. "Now, boys!" William instructed. "But don't you shoot any of my geese!"

All three of the mighty hunters took sight on a goose and pulled the trigger. They were so excited and so nervous that all three of them missed on the first shot. By the time they realized that they had missed, it was too late. The geese had taken to the sky and were totally gone in no time.

"That's a good start," William encouraged them. "They're pretty far out there. Just don't get in any hurry. Take it easy. There will be more pretty soon. There's a lot of them moving today."

The rest of the day and the rest of that week turned out to be much more successful. When the next geese landed, all three men were successful in bringing one down into the water. After the other geese took off, William himself waded out into the knee-deep water and retrieved their three dead geese. He carried them into the trees where the mule was tied and put them into the wagon. During the course of that day, the three great hunters killed thirty-two geese. They ended the day feeling very proud of themselves.

Over the next three days, the same schedule presented itself. On Tuesday, they killed thirty-four geese. On Wednesday, it rained very hard all day, and the take was only eighteen. Thursday was clear and cool, and the geese were everywhere. By the end of the day, they had killed forty-five and now had a total kill of one hundred and twenty-nine.

William told them that if that was enough, they could take the geese to a little place called New Holland and have them packed in dry ice and put on the train. He said that the geese would likely be home before Daddy, Hawkins, and Rippetoe got there on Sunday. And the geese would be well preserved. Then he had another idea for Friday. Everyone agreed.

On Friday morning, Mr. Campbell drove them to New Holland in his truck. It wasn't more than fifteen miles to the tiny town that was established when there had been an attempt to drain Lake Mattamuskeet and farm the rich land like the Dutch did with dikes in Holland. But it was too hard to keep the water out, and the plan did not last very long. Daddy told us that when he heard

Back in Waynesville after the big hunting trip. Posed photo with Canada geese that were shipped (uncleaned) back on dry ice on the train.

this story he was glad the dikes didn't work or they would not have had the lake for the hunting trip.

The geese were dispatched by train, and the men were returned to the supervision of William by late morning. He was ready for them with his new plan for the day. They were going to go out on the Pamlico Sound and rake up some oysters to eat.

They got into a heavy wooden boat that had a flat bottom and was about sixteen or eighteen feet long. The three men sat in the boat while William rowed it out into the sound. After a while, they got to where he was going, and he dropped an anchor made out of a cement block. Then William started using a long-handled kind of rake to pull up the oysters. Daddy said it looked like a potato digger but had double handles like a post-hole digger. It could grasp the oysters and then close up so they could be pulled to the top.

As soon as the first batch came up, William showed them how to take a short, thick knife and open the oysters up. He also showed them how to swallow the oysters and eat them whole and raw. I did ask Daddy if he liked the oysters. He told me, "Son, I did swallow some of those things, but then I gave mine back to the water so fast that if they could have found their own shells they might have crawled back in and lived." I took that to mean that he was not taken by the oysters. Rippetoe seemed to like them, he said, but Hawkins thought about as much of them as Daddy did.

When they had first dropped the anchor at the oyster beds, Daddy told us, it looked like the land was standing still and the boat was going up and down. After a while, however, it came to look like the boat was sitting still and the land was going up and down. (He did not tell me whether any alcohol was involved in this transition.) In no time, more than the swallowed oysters was donated to the Pamlico Sound, and the three fellows were ruined for the day.

Way out there in the Pamlico Sound, they could see some more land way across the water. Daddy wondered what and where that might be, so he asked William.

"That is a place called Ocracoke," William replied. "We don't want to go over there. That is where the wild people live!"

Daddy had no idea than one day one of his sons would call Ocracoke Island home.

As they started back toward the land in Swan Quarter, a big white swan suddenly came flying over the boat. Without saying anything at all, Hawkins grabbed his gun and shot the swan. It came falling down into the water.

William was terribly upset. "We don't shoot no swans," he quickly told the party. "Besides, that is against the law. Quick, we've got to find that thing and bury it way out of sight."

That is exactly what they did.

Everyone was glad to be back at the Campbells' house for the hot dinner on Friday night, William included. In the morning, it would be time to start for home.

Early on Saturday morning, the three great hunters got up for their last big breakfast with the Campbells. The Campbells had

William come over for breakfast also so they could say goodbye to him. All in all, they had had a wonderful adventure.

When the three of them went out to load the Hudson after breakfast, they saw that a large puddle of motor oil had run out from under the car and was almost soaked into the gravel where it was parked. Luckily, they saw it before trying to start the car. There was no oil at all showing on the dipstick. Daddy crawled under the car and found that they had blown out part of the gasket around the oil pan and that the majority of the motor oil had leaked out.

They appealed to the Campbells for advice about what to do. There was no mechanical help to be had in Swan Quarter, but they suggested a plan. The hunters were given the name of a man named Simmons who did mechanical work in Belhaven, along with directions about how to find him. The suggestion was to fill the car with oil and then to stop about every fifteen minutes and check the oil to see how fast it was leaking and then keep feeding it until they got safely to Belhaven. It was less than thirty miles, and the Campbells were sure they could make it safely.

They filled the car with oil and started. Daddy said that they actually drove only five minutes and then got out to check it. They were not taking any chances. Next, they drove ten minutes. After two twenty-minute drives and the addition of only a quart of oil, they were at the home of Mr. Simmons in Belhaven.

Daddy was glad to meet Mr. Simmons, as Daddy's own middle name was Simmons. There was likely a naming connection, they discovered, as Daddy had gotten his middle name from a man named Furnifold Simmons, who was in the legislature with his father. Furnifold Simmons came from New Bern, not very far from Belhaven.

Mr. Simmons was glad to help them even on a Saturday. He got under the Hudson and took off the oil pan. After he cleaned it up, he placed the oil pan on a large piece of cork and drew around it with a pencil. Then he took his sharp pocketknife and carefully cut out a gasket from the cork. Daddy said Mr. Simmons put some greasy-looking stuff on both sides of the gasket and put it in place. Then he tightened it up, and the Hudson was as good as new. The charge was four dollars.

Daddy added up his expenses and his money. Hawkins and Rippetoe had paid for the gas, since Daddy had brought his car. But they had divided both the room and the meals for the night in Durham on the way. They had each paid a total of ten dollars a day for five days for room and board and the hunting, plus the charge for shipping the geese back to Waynesville, and now they had to get back home. He was worried about running out of cash.

He said to Mr. Simmons, "Would it be possible to write you a check?"

Mr. Simmons smiled. "You mean a check with my own name on it? I have always wanted a check with my own name on it. I would be delighted if you wrote me a check."

Daddy wrote Mr. Simmons a check for five dollars, and Mr. Simmons never cashed it! He must have kept it for a souvenir as his first-ever personal check.

Now, after the repairs, the three were off for home. They decided to drive back the same way they had come and to spend Saturday night at the Jack Tar in Durham, since they already knew how to do that. They might even get there in time to see Daddy's brother Lee again.

It was November 2, 1929, when they drove into Durham. As they drove up to the Jack Tar Hotel, the whole world seemed to be astir. There had been no news for the week while they were in Swan Quarter. Now, here in Durham, all everyone wanted to do was talk in panic about the news.

On Thursday, October 24, while they were loading up to leave Waynesville to go goose hunting, the New York stock market had had a very rocky day and had ended down in value. If they had heard a little bit about this on the news, they had paid it no attention, as none of them owned any stocks at all and all the people who did were just getting richer and richer anyway. When Daddy had gone to the bank to take money out of savings for the trip, not a word had been mentioned about the stock market. People in Waynesville, North Carolina, had no imagination that what happened in New York City might have an effect on them.

During the week while they were hunting at Lake Mattamuskeet, there had been no mention of the news by the Campbells or by anyone else around Swan Quarter. They did not know that all during that week the value of stocks had continued to tumble. The market went down 13 percent while they were hunting on Monday. While they were shooting geese on Tuesday, stocks in New York went down another 12 percent. By the time the week ended and they got back to Durham, the entire country was in a panic, and the whole market economy seemed to be coming apart. It was the beginning of the twelve years we now call the Great Depression.

They did find Uncle Lee and take him out to eat. They were the only people eating in the Jack Tar dining room that night.

The next day, they drove on back to Waynesville.

On Monday, Daddy was back at work at the rag mill. That afternoon, the three men went to the train station and picked up their one hundred and twenty-nine geese. They even posed with the geese and had their photo made by Kelly's Studio.

It was fortunate for Daddy that he worked at Royal and Pilkington. They made very expensive drapery and upholstery material that they sold to interior decorators, mostly in New York City. Their product was so expensive that their work held up through those Depression years, as it continued to be bought by those few people who were wealthy enough to try to show to the world that they had not lost all of their money.

On the other end of things, the bank where Daddy had his savings closed before the end of 1929. It never occurred to him to try to go take his money out. The fifteen hundred dollars that he did not spend on the hunting trip were lost and gone forever.

Nearly a dozen years later, Daddy went to work for First National Bank in Waynesville. This was not the bank where he had lost his money. No, First National had stayed open. But in spite of working for the bank for the rest of his work life, Daddy never recovered his interest in saving money. Mama never could get him to save. She was the one who saved and who finally enabled me to go to college. Daddy spent it all. More than once, I heard him say, "If you want something and you have enough money to get it, you had better go on and get it now. You never can tell what is going to happen next week, and you may not be able to count on what you have now."

It took me a number of years to realize the connection between the hunting trip and Daddy's financial philosophy, but it finally made sense. It also made sense to me whenever I needed to justify an expenditure!

The Principal

It was at the dinner table the evening after my first week at school in the first grade. We were all eating and talking about that great week that could never be repeated again. Daddy had told about his first week of school, when his older brother Grover was his teacher. Mama had told about her first week of school, when she walked by herself over a mile to go to Fines Creek School, the first of nine sisters and brothers to do so.

When it was my turn, I thought my experiences at Hazelwood were thin compared to theirs. Mama had taken me to school, and together we recounted the week.

When we finished our report, Daddy looked at me and asked the question, "Have you met the principal?"

It was a trick question. I had never heard the word *principal* and had no idea what it meant.

"I don't know if I did or not," I shot back. "I don't know what the principal is. Tell me about it."

With Daddy on a family visit, age seven

Now, the principal of Hazelwood was Mr. Lawrence Leatherwood, my parents' good friend and one of our neighbors. I, however, had no idea that Mr. Leatherwood spent time at Hazelwood or that *principal* was his title. I thought his title was *Larry and Ronnie's daddy.*

My daddy smiled and attempted to answer my question. "Let's see, what's the best way to explain it? How about this: the principal is the person who takes care of you at school."

With that, I knew the answer to his question. "It's Mrs. Annie Ledbetter. She takes care of me!"

Mrs. Annie Ledbetter was a substantially built woman who had five dresses. Pants had never touched her legs. There was a Monday dress, a Tuesday dress, a Wednesday dress, a Thursday dress, and a Friday dress. If she had worn the dresses in chromatic order, it would have helped us learn the color spectrum. But no, she wore them from dull on Monday to red on Friday.

We loved it when red-dress day came each week. Then we knew for sure that we would not have to come to school on the next day. The red dress was the same color that all fire trucks were back then. It was made of a loosely knitted material so it could go in and out with the tide as it needed to through the course of the year. And it had tiny, raised white stripes that ran up and down and back and forth across the dress.

It was on this very day, the Friday of our first week at school, that we had seen the red dress for the first time. When Mrs. Ledbetter stood in front of us to call the roll, she was beautiful. Eddie Curtis was so overwhelmed that he could not contain himself! When his name was called, he was not content to simply answer, "Present." No, he could not help himself. "Oh, Mrs. Ledbetter," Eddie went on, "I do just love that dress! It makes you look just like a big brick building!"

Mrs. Ledbetter burst out laughing before any of the rest of us even started. She doubled over with laughter, she laughed until tears were coming down her face, and she laughed louder and longer than any of the rest of us!

Something inside of me knew that if we had a teacher who could laugh like that, she was someone who would always take care of us, so she must be the principal! What else could the answer have been?

"The principal is Mrs. Annie Ledbetter!"

"Oh, no, son," Daddy came back. "She's not the principal, she's just your teacher. I heard that she got the *A*s through the *G*rs this year. She only takes care of your first-grade class, not everybody."

Well, I thought, *she takes care of me, and that is all that matters.*

"Then what is the principal anyway?" I tried the question again.

"Think about it like this." Daddy looked thoughtful. "Mrs. Ledbetter takes care of your class, and there are other teachers who take care of their classes. You are right about this, but the principal is not one of the teachers. Instead, the principal has the special job of taking overall care of every single one of the students in all of the classes."

I listened carefully, then thought for a moment. Now, I knew the answer: the principal had to be Mrs. Calhoun!

Mrs. Calhoun lived in the lunchroom. We all knew that she lived there because she had never been sighted anywhere in town outside of that space. And we all could see that sun had never touched her skin. Her complexion was the same color as the white government-surplus lard and the white government-surplus flour that made up the bulk of what we got to eat at school. And when you added her white industrial-strength hairnet, her white uniform, and her white crepe-soled shoes, she was one color from top to bottom!

Every single day of the school year, Mrs. Calhoun made fresh, homemade yeast rolls. By ten in the morning, you could take in the wonderful smell of the yeast rolls as it wafted from one end of the school halls to the other.

It was always a treat to be sent to do an errand in the morning when she was making yeast rolls. That meant that you got to cut through the lunchroom and peek a bit at Mrs. Calhoun as she was in the middle of roll production. It was a sight to linger over and watch for a few minutes. Mrs. Calhoun had a large and heavy metal bowl that was bigger than a good-sized dishpan. I had never seen a container that large. It had a rounded bottom and held a seeming mountain of yeast-roll dough. It was the daily incubation center for these delicious rolls.

There it would be on the school kitchen counter, the huge bowl filled with living yeast dough. Mrs. Calhoun would have her hands plunged deeply into the dough. She was so nearly the same color and the same soft, fluffy consistency as the dough that it was impossible to tell where the dough started and Mrs. Calhoun stopped. She had big, flabby upper arms that dangled and wiggled as she worked the dough; everything in sight seemed to be flopping up and down.

Mrs. Calhoun would somehow loop her arm around a big strand of yeast dough, squeeze the end between her thumb and forefinger, and—*plop!*—a roll-sized piece of dough would land right in the proper spot on the greased baking pan. Then she went back and forth a row at a time until the pan was filled. Once a pan was occupied with uncooked rolls, she would paint the tops of them with a paintbrush she dipped into a pan of melted government-surplus butter and slide the pan into a huge oven that had the name Blodgett in red letters on its door.

If you got to stick around, you would get to see her repeat the process and continue to pull out the beautiful golden brown, heavenly smelling yeast rolls and follow them with more pans of new rolls to be baked. It was an everyday operation. All the way back in the classroom, even the teachers could detect the wonderful aroma. At that time, if a teacher determined that some child in the class had come to school without breakfast that day, the teacher would slip up to him or her and quietly direct, "Honey, why don't you go see Mrs. Calhoun for a few minutes." That child would return to the classroom a short time later with a big, hot roll that had butter melting and dripping from its edges, and his or her entire life would be improved from that moment forward.

So, I thought, *if the principal is the person who takes care of everybody, how could it be any person other than dear Mrs. Calhoun?*

So I proclaimed to Daddy, "I know the principal. It's Mrs. Calhoun!"

"No," he chuckled. "I know Mrs. Calhoun. She's the lunchroom lady. No, son, you still don't have it right."

Now, I was confused more than ever. "Okay," I started, "tell me all over again. What is the principal supposed to be?"

Daddy smiled at me. "The principal is in charge of everything—both the students and the teachers. The principal is like the king of the school and the president of the school all at the same time. The principal is in charge of the school buses, the buildings, the playground, the lunchroom, the teachers, the students. Why, the principal is even in charge of the bathrooms!"

After that description, I was sure that I now knew the right answer. "You can't fool me anymore," I told Daddy. "The principal is Haskell Davis."

Haskell Davis was actually my daddy's cousin. He weighed about ninety-five pounds soaking wet. About ninety pounds of that was red hair and freckles. Haskell had more freckles than anyone had ever seen. He had freckles beside freckles, freckles above and below freckles, and even freckles hiding behind other freckles so they could show up just in case the ones in front didn't come to work that day.

Everyone called Haskell "Hack," and he was always the first person we saw when we arrived at school each morning. Hack always stood at the front door of the school and held the door open for us as we entered the building under his outstretched arm.

Hack knew everyone, and as we passed under his arm he would greet each of us by our last name: "Hello, little Rathbone. Hello, little Messer. Hello, little Ferguson. Hello, little Davis. Feel my muscle, feel my muscle!" We would each reach up as we passed under his arm and touch his clenched bicep. Even though Haskell weighed only ninety-five pounds, he had a bicep that was like a five-pound ball bearing.

After we touched Hack's rock-hard bicep, we each knew we were going to behave all day, because he was the one we knew to be in charge of the school. Besides that, Haskell had the amazing and marvelous power of multiple simultaneous physical location. He could be out at the bus stop and inside in the boys' bathroom at the same time. He could be in the lunchroom and at the far end of the entire building both at once. He seemed to be always everywhere.

And if that were not enough, Haskell had to be the principal because he was in charge of the throw-up compound. The throw-up compound looked like dark red, oily sawdust and had the smell of very ripe bananas combined with motor oil. Haskell kept it in a large fiber barrel in a closet on the main school hallway.

We did not have 911 in those days, so when there was an emergency the teacher simply opened the door of the classroom and yelled, "Has-kell!" He could tell from the tone of voice exactly what the trouble was.

Here Hack would come, trotting down the hall, a dustpan filled with throw-up compound in one hand and a little broom with a sawed-off handle in the other. He would sweep into the room, spot the offense, scatter the reddish compound all over it, sweep it together and into the dustpan, and, like magic, he was gone! (One day, we even heard him tell one of our teachers that it was good for more than just throw-up. "It works just as well on blood and boogers," he whispered to her.)

So Haskell had to be the principal. I could not be wrong again.

"No," Daddy replied, "Haskell's not the principal. He's the janitor. We would call him the custodian, but I don't think Haywood County can afford four syllables."

I was totally dismayed. I knew that Haskell had to be the principal because he was surely the king and the president of the school. "I give up," I conceded to Daddy. "I don't know. You are just going to have to tell me who the principal is."

"It's Mr. Leatherwood, our neighbor."

I couldn't believe this. "Mr. Leatherwood?" I queried. "I haven't even seen him at school. How could he be the principal?"

I must have looked both disappointed and discouraged, and Daddy must have realized that he shouldn't leave our consultation open at this point. He seemed to think for a few moments. Then he sat down and pulled me onto his lap.

"Actually," he started, "all of your guesses were as good as they could be. You know that titles like *principal, teacher, janitor, lunchroom lady* don't make any difference in the long run anyway. Even titles like *king* and *president* don't mean anything all by themselves."

He was sounding serious now. "Here's how it really works: every single person you meet gets one of two titles way back in the back of your brain without your even having to think about it. Those two titles are *someone who will help me* and *someone who could hurt me*. Now, you think about that for a minute."

I knew without thinking that he was right. All of the kids in my first-grade school class fell easily into one of those two categories. All of my relatives could be divided in the same way. In fact, every person of every age that I could think of could be labeled the same way. How did my daddy know this?

He started talking again, this time looking far away and not at all at me. "What we need to learn, son, is to spend as much time as we can with those people who will help us and as little time as possible with those people who could hurt us. And when we look in the mirror at ourselves, we need to try to be sure that we are looking at a person whom others will always know will help them."

As I was falling asleep that night, a very strange thought came to me. I had just spent a whole week at school, the place where I was supposed to go to learn things. But in about fifteen minutes, my own father had taught me more than I had learned in school in that whole week.

The Cigarette

Whenever I did something that I knew was wrong, and I knew that Daddy knew about it, I almost looked forward to getting the punishment over with so that it could be forgotten. The problem was that Daddy didn't like to do it this way. He was more interested in learning, more interested in memory, than in pure punishment.

Instead of punishment, I would often hear these words: "Let me tell you a little story!"

I came to hate those words as a response to my own wrongdoing. I wanted the punishment to come quickly and then be over with. The stories lasted a longer time in the telling, and I could not get it out of my mind after I had heard one.

The bank where Daddy worked was open each day from nine to one for business. The bank closed at one so that the tellers and loan officers could now become the bookkeepers. They would spend the afternoon entering the work they had done during "banker's hours" and making sure that all of the entries balanced on the books. As the cashier and later vice president of the bank, Daddy had to stay until everyone balanced. Part of his job was to make sure that the overall business of the day was in order.

We had supper at our house at five o'clock each day. By that time, they had either balanced at the bank or Daddy would have to go back and work into the night until all was in order. I still remember times when he would come home for supper and say to Mama, "Lucille, we are out eighteen cents. I know that it is an entry inversion"—someone had entered, for example, thirteen cents rather than thirty-one—"because the error is divisible by nine. I have to go back until we find it."

Mama would reply, "Can't you just put in eighteen cents out of your pocket and come on home?"

"No, Lucille, the bank examiners have to find us in perfect order when they come. We have our reputation to take care of!"

Part of what this overall system meant was that, after one o'clock in the afternoon, there were no customers for Daddy to deal with at the bank. No, he, too, was doing entry and balance work related to the loan operations he was in charge of. So Mama knew that it would not be bothering his work with customers if she left me at the bank in his care while she went places when she wanted no interference from a little boy. Whenever she had to go to the doctor, do certain kinds of shopping, or go to the beauty parlor, I would be dropped off at the bank, where Daddy was my passive babysitter.

One day, Mama left me at the bank while she went for her semester at the Ladye Faire Beauty Parlor. I spent an interesting afternoon rolling coins and adding phone numbers. It was a day when everyone balanced with no problems, so before five o'clock it was time for everyone to go home. Today was Daddy's day to lock up at the bank, so everyone else had now left and he was doing the final checking and preparation for the lockup.

The last task before actually going out the door was for Daddy

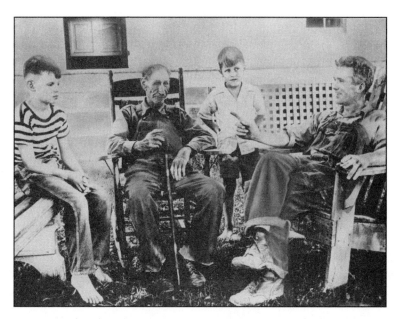

Uncle Frank (*right*) swapping stories with neighbor Silas Jolly. Between them stands my cousin Phillips. On the left is one of the Medford neighbors.

to wind the time clocks in the back of the door of the big Mosler bank vault. Everyone at the bank was proud of the Mosler vault. Daddy told me that the actual Declaration of Independence and the real Constitution were locked up in a Mosler vault in Washington, D.C.

The vault had a huge silver door. There were shiny bars that slid into the sides of the door when you turned a wheel that looked like the steering wheel of a ship. It was beautiful.

Daddy would open the vault door, then open a glass panel on the back of that door. There were three time clocks attached to the locking mechanism. Once they were wound and set for eight o'clock the next morning, no one could open the vault door even if they knew the exact combination.

It took a few minutes to carry out this operation and then close and lock the big silver door. While he was out of sight winding the clocks, I had time to engage in one of my favorite hobbies: snooping and prowling. Now, no one else at all was in the bank except Daddy, and he was occupied.

One of the men who worked at the bank was Mr. Jack Way. Mr. Way was a friendly man who was also the perpetual mayor of Waynesville. He had a big desk near the front of the lobby, and his main job seemed to be to visit and talk with people as they came in and out of the bank. Mr. Way dressed well and was the only man I had ever seen who wore a diamond ring on his pinkie finger. He was a curiosity.

Mr. Way always kept a big fishbowl on his desk that was filled with Juicy Fruit chewing gum and small Tootsie Rolls. He would pass them out to children who happened to come into the bank with their parents. He usually offered me Juicy Fruit gum, which I did not like. I wanted Tootsie Rolls.

I was just looking at the gum and candy in the fishbowl, not touching it or planning to touch it at all. That is when I saw something else on top of his desk. It was an open and partially empty pack of Cavalier cigarettes. I don't think that Mr. Way smoked. Some customer must have accidently left it there.

I did not do it! No, you are not responsible for what your hands do when you are seven or eight years old. All on their own, one of my hands decided that it wanted one of those cigarettes. I simply watched it happen as my hand picked up the cigarette pack, shook a cigarette out onto the desktop, picked it up, and put it into my shirt pocket. Now, I could not get it out! I had to go home with it.

Daddy came out of the vault, closed the big silver door, spun the big wheel that slid the bars into their holes, and twirled the knobs of the combination locks. "That's it for today!" he exclaimed. "Let's go home."

Mama had supper on the table when we walked in the door. The cigarette was about to burn its own hole in my pocket. It would have to wait until after we ate. I was finished in no time but had to wait until everyone was through eating before I could politely be excused.

As soon as we were all finished, I said to my brother, Joe, "Let's go out and play in the barn loft. I know something good we can do." Mama said nothing, as she was glad to have us out of the way while she cleaned up and she and Daddy washed and dried the dishes.

The barn loft was one of our favorite playing places. It was a small barn for our one milk cow, Helen. There were two stalls in the back and a feed room on the side. The other quarter of the little barn was simply an overhang where Daddy usually milked the cow. The stairs to the loft went up from the feed room.

We kept hay for Helen in the barn loft. Daddy would buy hay from some local farmer, who would bring it and toss it up through the door on the front of the loft. Joe and I thought the rectangular bales of hay were our play toys. We treated them like giant building blocks and made tunnels and castles and hideouts of all kinds as the hay gradually disappeared through the course of winter feeding. There were two holes in the floor that went straight down to the mangers in the stalls, so you could drop down the right amount when it was needed.

It was not unusual for us to play in the barn loft, so neither Joe nor our parents gave any thought at all to my suggestion that we go there.

Once up in the loft, I pulled out the cigarette. "Look what I got!" I proudly showed it to Joe. I put the cigarette in my mouth as I talked to him, letting it flop up and down the way I had seen Humphrey Bogart do in the movies. Joe had such an admiring look on his face that I knew I was doing a good job of showing off.

From here on out, everything that happened was his fault.

Joe smiled at me and said, "Smoke it, smoke it, smoke it!"

I was not planning on smoking it. I did not know how to smoke it. I did not even know whether to suck in or blow out to make the cigarette smoke. All I was doing was showing off. But challenged by my little brother, I had to try.

Somehow, there were matches in my pocket! I took out the little box and got ready to strike a match, still not knowing exactly what to do. Just as I struck the match, we heard Daddy coming from the house toward the barn to milk the cow. He was singing as he came. Daddy loved to sing, and he always sang as he worked in the garden or milked the cow or did any other jobs around the house. Most of his songs were old church songs or Hank Williams. He was singing an old church song as we first heard him: "Why should I feel discouraged . . . ?"

"Hide it, hide it, hide it!" Joe whispered loudly the moment we heard Daddy singing.

I was way ahead of him. I had already blown out the match and dropped it on the floor of the barn loft. What to do with the cigarette? Again, my hands took over. They took the cigarette from my mouth, balled it up, and stuffed it down into a wide crack between two boards in the floor of the barn loft.

The crack looked like it had a bottom to it. But what looked like a bottom was simply an accumulation of old hay trash and dust. As soon as I pushed the wadded cigarette into the crack, I was pushing the hay trash out the bottom. All of the hay trash, the dust, and the wadded cigarette fell right through the crack and went streaming down to the ground just as Daddy arrived to milk Helen. He was finishing the song: "His eye is on the sparrow, and I know he *watches* me." For some strange reason, he did not even notice the falling debris.

Joe and I held our breath—we almost held our heartbeats—as we hunkered silently right above where he was preparing to milk the cow. We could actually watch through the same now-open crack as he gave Helen a scoop of dairy mash cow food, pulled up his milking stool, washed her udder with the warm, wet cloth he had brought for that. We watched and listened as he milked, from the first long and heavy streams hitting the bucket until the last thin squirts when he was finishing. He did not sing anymore while he milked. We stayed frozen in place as he put Helen into her stall for the night and carried the bucket of milk back to the house.

Joe and I breathed sighs of relief as we eased down the barn-loft steps and circled our way back to the house. Mama was straining the milk in the kitchen when we walked in the door.

"Well," I said nervously, "it's about to get dark now. I reckon it is about time for us to stop playing outdoors and come inside for the night."

Joe agreed.

Mama offered us some ice cream before we went to bed. "You boys were in such a hurry to go outside after supper that you didn't even wait for me to offer you some dessert. You can have it now."

I was not hungry at all, but I eagerly agreed and silently ate the ice cream.

In a little while, Mama made the regular announcement: "Well, boys, it is a school night. It's about time to get on your pajamas and think about bed. You boys wash your hands and feet before you get in the clean beds."

"Aw," Joe whined. He always did this. "I am just not sleepy. I don't want to go to bed."

Before there was time for Mama even to think about her reply to Joe's argument, Daddy jumped into the conversation. "So, if you don't want to go to bed yet, why don't I tell you a little story?" He looked at Mama for agreement. "Surely, there's time for that, Lucille."

She smiled agreement. "I think that would be fine, as long as it's not too long. What story are you thinking about telling tonight? You know I always love the one about the pet squirrels."

"Not that one this time," he went on. "I was thinking I might tell about the time that Frank and Harry burned Little Joe Medford's barn down. How about that one?" Daddy loved to tell us stories about things that he and his brothers had done when they were our age.

Mama looked surprised. "I don't think I have ever heard that one. What is it about, Joe?"

"It's a good story." Daddy smiled. "You will all like it." And he started, "I guess that Frank and Harry were about the same age that Donald and Joe are now." And the story unfolded before us.

Our grandfather, Daddy's father, was running for the state

legislature (where he served for the last three decades of his life). One afternoon, a man from Waynesville had come out to the farm to talk with him about politics. They sat in the kitchen so they could drink coffee, and they talked at the kitchen table all afternoon.

After they finished their talking and the man went on his way home, Frank and Harry were poking around in the kitchen, getting something to drink. They noticed that the man had left something on the table and that their father had not noticed it. It was an open pack of Camel cigarettes. This was a real curiosity, as at that time almost every smoker rolled his own cigarettes. The manufactured cigarettes were something they had never seen before, let alone touched!

Before anyone could come along and catch then, the two boys grabbed the pack of cigarettes, got some wooden matches, and headed out of the house. Without even having to talk about it, they were automatically looking for a place where they could smoke a cigarette.

Daddy went on with the story: "They thought about climbing up into the barn loft and smoking up there. But they decided that would be dangerous, since Daddy might go out to milk and catch them."

He went on to tell us about how his brothers Frank and Harry had gone up the hill behind their house, then continued on over the hill and down the other side to where Little Joe Medford lived. Once they got over to Little Joe's place, they climbed up into the loft of his barn, and in no time they were puffing on one of those cigarettes and passing it back and forth between them.

All of a sudden, they heard someone coming. It was Little Joe himself, coming out to his own barn to milk the cow. Frank said to Harry, "Hide it, hide it, hide it!" By the time it was said, Harry had mashed the cigarette down into a crack between two wide boards in the floor of the barn loft and the boys had jumped down out of the back of that loft.

Little Joe saw the two of them run off, but he didn't really think much about it. These two boys were all over the country all the time anyway. He went on into the barn and milked his cow, then turned her back out into the pasture, since it was a warm spring night.

Daddy's face got serious as he got to this part of the story. "Well, boys," he went on slowly, "way in the night, that cigarette smoldered around and came back to life. Harry had not actually been sure that it was out, since he was in such a hurry to hide it. Finally, the dust ignited, then the hay trash caught on fire, then the hay in the barn loft caught on fire, then the entire barn was on fire. Since it was in the middle of the night, no one knew that it was burning until it came popping and crackling through the roof, and by then it was too late for Little Joe to do anything but watch it burn and hope that it didn't set anything else on fire. It was a good thing it was a warm night and there were no animals shut up inside."

Joe could not stay quiet any longer. "What happened then?" he asked, fear in his voice. "Did Uncle Frank and Uncle Harry get caught?"

"I'll tell you boys all that I know about it," Daddy went on. "Since Little Joe had seen those two boys jump down out of the barn loft and run off, he knew who had started the fire. And by now, Mama had found the rest of the cigarettes when she gathered up the dirty clothes to wash and cleaned out Frank's pockets. Before it was all over, Daddy had to build Little Joe a new barn. And he had to pay for it. I do not know what went on between Daddy and Frank and Harry. That was between the three of them. Then again, I didn't want to know about it. It might have been pretty bad, I imagine."

We just sat there in silence.

Daddy finally spoke: "Well, boys, what do you think of that story?"

Joe was quick to answer, but it was with a question: "Is it all right for us to go to bed now?"

And that is exactly what we did.

That was all that was ever said about the whole cigarette business. Mama sent us to bed looking like she did not at all understand why Daddy had chosen to tell us that particular story that night. But Joe and I clearly knew several things. We knew that Daddy knew. We knew that he had practiced the wonderful grace of not catching us openly and creating an embarrassing scene that would also have involved Mama. We also knew that he had given us one chance—and that we had better not try it again.

Fontana
National Bank

In May of 1933, President Franklin Roosevelt signed the bill creating the Tennessee Valley Authority as one of the major economic recovery projects of the New Deal. The TVA, as it was called, eventually built twenty-nine dams in the valleys of the Tennessee River watershed, providing both flood control and power in a large part of the nation that was especially depressed economically.

On the eve of World War II, the Alcoa aluminum company in Alcoa, Tennessee, was in the process of negotiating with the TVA to build a large dam to enable it to step up aluminum production for wartime readiness. Following the bombing of Pearl Harbor and America's entry into the war, on December 17, 1941 (just ten days after the Japanese surprise bombing), Congress authorized the building of the Fontana Dam under emergency wartime initiatives. This was to be the highest dam ever built east of the Rockies and would produce power not only for Alcoa but also for the secret atomic research of the Manhattan Project in Oak Ridge, Tennessee.

The Fontana Dam site was located on the Little Tennessee River west of the small town of Bryson City in the mountains of western North Carolina. It was seventy-two miles, part still on unpaved roads, from the town of Waynesville to the Fontana Dam construction site.

I was never told how the arrangement was actually made. Were there no closer banks to the construction site, or did First National Bank in Waynesville have more capital? However it happened, the bank in which Daddy went to work in 1941 at the end of that same year secured a special arrangement with the TVA, and he was placed in charge of that project.

On each Friday, the overall paymaster at the dam site would call Daddy at the bank and tell him what the payroll for the week was. The building of the dam involved over six thousand people, from officials and supervisors to engineers and workmen and the families they brought to the site with them. They all lived in and worked from a quickly built construction camp that provided not only housing but cafeterias, a hospital, a theater, churches, recreation buildings, and a school for dependent children. The work started in January of 1942.

After the phone message came in telling Daddy what the payroll for the week was, he would pull his 1936 Plymouth up to the front door of the bank and park it half on the sidewalk with the trunk open. Then, with the bank door propped open, he could trek back and forth between the Mosler vault and the Plymouth's trunk until he had loaded enough currency in the back of the car to cover the payroll.

Once loaded, he climbed into the Plymouth and headed for Fontana. The road went through Maggie Valley and up over Soco Mountain. It continued through Cherokee and Bryson City and around the site of the coming lake until he arrived at the large construction village. Finally there, he would spend the night in a little guest house with all of that cash in the trunk of the Plymouth

Daddy as he looked forever

that was parked just outside. After a good night of sleep, he would move the car down to a little building near the store, unload the currency, and open what he described as "a little Saturday-morning storefront bank."

The dam site was so far from where most of the laborers called home that very few of them left on the weekends, since most had their families there living with them. Besides the school and the churches and a clinic, there were even square dances on Saturday night for weekend entertainment. So almost no one went away to where there was a bank either to deposit their checks or cash them. Daddy had a very large group of clients. He stayed open from nine until one on Saturday, the same hours that the bank in Waynesville stayed open each weekday. It seemed the right thing to do.

During his business hours, he opened accounts for people and deposited their checks into their new accounts. For some people, he cashed their entire check. The checks were good, and what they intended to do with their money was not his business. For most of his Fontana customers, he deposited their checks as they held out a small amount of cash to make it through the coming week. This meant that when he closed the little bank on Saturday afternoon, he still had the bulk of the currency he had brought with him for the business day. He was committed to having enough money theoretically to cash all of the checks, so he brought an amount equal to the total payroll. Now, he loaded more than half of what he had brought back into the Plymouth, where it would be with him until he returned to work on Monday.

On Saturday afternoon, he got in the loaded Plymouth and drove all the way back to Waynesville. He told me that he often picked up hitchhikers on the way because he knew that many people had no cars in the mountains in those days.

Back at home, the Plymouth sat in our driveway with all that cash (and the deposit and withdrawal records) in the trunk for the rest of the weekend. The money traveled to church and back on Sunday. It often traveled to my grandmother's house for a Sunday-afternoon visit. It often went to see his brother Grover or brother Frank or sisters Mary and Esther. No thought at all was given to there being any danger to either him or the money.

On Monday morning, he went back to work at the bank. On these days, he would drive the car up to the Main Street door and pull one set of tires up on the sidewalk to get it farther out of the street. He then went inside, opened the door of the weekend-locked Mosler vault, and made as many trips as were necessary to bring all the cash and paperwork into the bank.

The same routine repeated itself for more than two and a half years until the dam was finished and the power plant opened in November of 1944.

Later in life when I would get him to tell me this story again, I had a question for him: "Did you ever feel like you were in danger or that somebody might rob you?"

His answer gave me surprise, insight into who he was, and personal learning. "Son," he told me on several occasions, "about all you have to worry about in life is whether you are doing the right thing. You can't worry about whether other people are doing the right thing. You can't manage them. If I had ever been robbed, the robber is the one who was doing what was wrong. It wasn't my job to worry about that."

Many years later, I was the victim of an armed robbery in Nashville, Tennessee. When I asked the policeman who was writing up the report if I was somehow in the wrong place at the wrong time, he could have learned his answer from my father. He put down his pen, looked at me with a comforting smile, and said, "Mister, it is against the law to rob somebody no matter where they are. No, you did not do anything wrong by being here." It was a caretaker's answer.

Sometime later, I had another question for my father: "Was there ever a weekend when you did not want to go?"

"Oh," he almost chuckled, "there was one time when I didn't go. It was the weekend when your mother and I got married! Jim Noland filled in and went for me that time."

I thought that was the end of his answer until I saw the almost pained look on his face and knew something else was coming.

"The time I wish I hadn't gone was the weekend after you were born. You were born on Thursday, and your mama had such a hard time that you were both in the hospital for weeks after that. But the day after you were born, I had to load up the money, leave both of you in the hospital in Waynesville, and go on over there. At the time, I kept telling myself that it had gotten to be too big a job to get anyone else to do it. I'll tell you right now, if I had it to do again, I wouldn't have gone, even if they had to go a week without a bank at Fontana."

From a man whose responsible dedication to his job was unbendable, this said more to me than if he had struggled to say, "I love you."

"See You Next Sunday!"

Daddy used to tell me that the hardest month of the year was April. This surprised me, as I thought the hardest months were surely January and February.

"No," he explained, "April is the month when all of the food that we put up for the year started to run out. Nothing was growing yet, and we wondered if this year we would live through April or starve. By May, we could gather greens and soon even could scrabble for small potatoes."

He was, of course, talking about his childhood. It was a time on the farm when new ground was still being cleared to make room to grow crops, mostly food to feed a family of ten children and at least three adults.

"The only thing we had to buy," he often told me, "was salt. That was so we could cure pork and pickle things. It wasn't so much because we liked salty food as it was for preservation through the winter. We raised every single thing that we ate and made everything that we wore or lived in."

The major daily agenda on the homesteading farm was not first of all, "What can we sell?" but before that, "How do we make a six-month growing season (at most) feed us all year?"

All through the summer months and into the fall, the family put up food for the winter. Potatoes were a mainstay. After they were dug and dried out, they were put into a hole in the ground and covered with straw and then dirt, where they would last the winter without freezing. Beans and peppers and apples were dried. Lots of things were canned using Ball jars with rubber rings and only a water-bath canner. Apples were a staple and were put in the barn by the bushel, where they were protected from freezing. Cabbages were buried in sawdust in bins in the barn.

Though a generation younger, Mama had grown up much the same way. In my childhood, her parents—my only living grandparents—were still putting things up in the old way.

So even though Daddy now worked in town at the bank and Mama was a schoolteacher, they lived in fear that there would not be enough to eat. After all, the Depression might come back, Mr. Roosevelt was no longer president, and we had to be able to feed ourselves no matter what happened in the false economic world.

That is the main reason we did not live in town. Daddy had owned a small house before he married Mama. The house was in town in Hazelwood. But we were not to live there. No, the moment they married, he sold that house and bought a house that was far enough out of town that we had several acres of usable land around it.

From my earliest memories, we had two huge gardens. Each one was practically half the size of a football field, it seemed to me. One was planted totally in corn and beans. Every few weeks of the growing season, Daddy would plant about four rows of Golden Cross Bantam sweet corn. When the corn was about a foot high, he would plant the next four rows of corn, then plant beans beside the corn that was already up. That way, the bean vines grew up the cornstalks and we picked both at nearly the same time.

The other half of the big garden was for everything else. There were lots of tomatoes, okra, and cucumbers. There was squash of several kinds, lima beans in multiple varieties, and more than one kind of onion grown in large quantities. Multiple pepper varieties were set out, as well as cabbages and even broccoli in later years. Early on, there was abundant leaf lettuce and a mixture of greens for cooking.

Between the two sides of the garden was a double row of at least a dozen apple trees of several kinds, from June apples to Stayman Winesaps.

We canned and canned and canned from the garden. I never did understand why we called it "canning" when it was "jarring." All through the summer, Mama and Daddy canned food in the evenings and on Saturdays. Joe and I were recruited to help. We did not cooperate as we were given jobs such as stringing and breaking beans, washing vegetables, and carrying things here and there. It was hard work.

The canning was done seven quarts at a time in a big pressure canner on the stove in the kitchen. It would be hot as blazes when things got going in there. We canned beans, corn, beets, apples, carrots, onions, pickled okra, pickled cucumbers of every kind, kraut, tomatoes, tomato juice, grape juice—the list went on and on.

All through the year, whenever Mama's sisters and their families came to visit, they went home with canned goods. They were schoolteachers from Florida to Illinois, and Mama was not sure that they could buy the kinds of food that they needed to eat in such foreign places. Of course, the gifts of canned food were attached to a strong promise to bring back the empty jars so they could be used again the next summer.

We always had chickens. Every spring, we ordered baby chicks through the mail. Everyone we knew also ordered their little chicks through the mail, and all the ordered chickens came to the post office in town on the same day. On that day, Mr. Bishop, the postmaster, would call everybody who had ordered chickens: "The chickens are here. Come and get your chickens. I don't want dead chickens in the post office."

Joe and I loved to go with Daddy to get the baby chicks at the post office. When we opened the post office door, the entire place sounded like a chicken house full of little chicks. *Cheep, cheep, cheep* echoed everywhere. Mr. Bishop would find the boxes with Daddy's name on them, and we would head home with a stack of chicken boxes in the trunk of our car.

The little chicks came shipped in large, flat boxes that had small, round holes around the edges. The little ones tried to stick their heads out of these little holes. When we got home with them, Daddy would find a large corrugated pasteboard box and put it in the middle of the kitchen floor. We would line the bottom of the box with many thicknesses of newspaper and pour the little chicks into the large box.

While we were helping Daddy do this, Mama hunted for the cord into which we could screw a light bulb. She found a forty-watt bulb that Daddy said was just the right replacement for the chicks' mamas. Once plugged in, the bulb dangled over the top of the box, adding a tiny bit of warmth to their new home. After this, we put a pie plate in the bottom with chicken feed in it and another pie plate with water in it and left the baby chicks for their first night in our family.

Early the next morning, Joe and I headed eagerly for the kitchen. It smelled awful! The baby chicks had somehow turned their water over into the food, then had walked around in it and pooped in it all night. It really made us want to skip breakfast.

We would keep the baby chicks in their kitchen box until they got big enough to fly up and out into the kitchen. Then it was time to take them out to the chicken house, where they would join the big chickens already living there. They would then grow up with the big chickens until they eventually began to lay eggs and become candidates for Mama's menus when she sent Daddy out to kill a chicken for her.

Every year, we ordered a different kind of chicken. One year we would get Rhode Island Reds, the next year we would get Plymouth Rocks, and the third year we would order Domineckers. Then we would start the cycle over again. The reason for changing breeds was so that Daddy could tell which hens were the oldest ones when Mama sent him out to kill one for her to cook. Of course, all of the small roosters were eaten first each year, then the hens got their turn for the pot.

Mama would greet Daddy when he came home from work: "Joe, I think I'll cook a chicken tonight. Would you go get me one?"

Daddy's only question was, "How do you want it cut up?" He needed to know whether it was to fry or bake or stew.

"Let's have it fried tonight," was her answer, and he was off. I would follow him out the door. Mama's last words to him were, "I've almost got the water boiling for you."

Daddy was fast. In no time, he would capture one of the older chickens. Before the chicken knew what was happening, her head was chopped off at the chopping block. Daddy would put the flopping chicken under a tin tub while he got the pot of boiling water Mama handed him from the back door.

Now that the chicken had stopped flopping, Daddy turned over the tub and scalded the chicken with boiling water so that its feathers came out easily as he plucked it. He would send me to get some newspaper. Once he plucked the chicken as cleanly as possible, Daddy would light a roll of newspaper and singe off the tiny pinfeathers that he could not pluck.

Quickly, he then gutted the chicken, took off its feet, and cut it up perfectly for Mama to fry for our supper. This meant that it was cut up with the wishbone (we called it "the pully-bone") intact: my favorite part!

We were never without a milk cow. Throughout most of my childhood, we had a sweet Jersey cow named Helen. Daddy said that he did not name the cow. No, he told us that the cow had been named Helen by her parents, and that you cannot change the name that someone's parents gave them.

Helen's name was an issue in our family because on Plott Creek Road, where we lived, we had nearby neighbors named the Burgins. Mrs. Burgin's name was Helen. Mama was very embarrassed that our cow had the same name as Mrs. Burgin.

In the backyard when I was two or three. Our cow, Helen, is in the back.

Daddy used the naming coincidence in the practice of his favorite hobby: annoying Mama. He would go out into our pasture to get our Helen to go to the barn for milking. Our cow pasture ran up the creek behind our house and behind the Burgins' house. Often, Mrs. Burgin would be sitting out on their back porch, looking out over the creek and the mountains. Daddy would check to be sure that Mama could hear him, then, in his loudest voice, he would say something like, "Oh, there you are, Helen. I was looking for you. I am ready for you. Come and meet me at the barn!"

Mama would flush with embarrassment. "Joe," she would call out, "you stop that! Can't you see Mrs. Burgin right there on the porch? She thinks that you are talking to her. Stop that right now!"

Daddy would laugh. (Mrs. Burgin probably also laughed!) "I can't help it if she doesn't know that she's not a cow," he would say.

Mama was so easy to embarrass.

We had a small barn that was Helen's winter home and the place where Daddy always milked her. It was maybe twenty-four feet on a side with two stalls in the back. In the front, there was a feed room on one side, and the other fourth was simply an open overhang. This was the milking place.

We always had one pig. The pig lived in a small and ancient-looking pigpen that was beyond the chicken house from the barn.

I never heard the word *recycle* as a child, but later on, when that became a popular word, the first thing that I thought of was our series of pigs from childhood. Everything that we did not eat we fed to the pig. The pig had no qualms about eating anything. Then we ate the pig.

I remember one night when we were having pork chops for supper. Daddy cut the fat off of the side of his pork chop and held it up on his fork. He looked at Mama and said, "Lucille, how many times do you reckon we have had these same pork chops?"

"Joe!" was all she said.

We spent so very much of our lives obsessed with food. It was simply assumed that we had to be able to feed ourselves without depending on either the grocery store or money for shopping.

Producing and putting up food was a way of life.

The summer after I was in the second grade, a great change came into our lives with respect to our ability to preserve food. Enabled by the North Carolina State Agriculture Extension Office, a cooperative community cannery was built behind the high school in town. When it was finished, it became possible for us to put our own food up in real cans—not seven quart jars at a time, but bushels at a time.

The cannery was a small, rectangular one-story block building. It was filled with bright stainless-steel equipment. There were wonderful, gigantic sinks for washing and cleaning food to be canned. There were big steam cookers where huge amounts of vegetables could be precooked before filling the cans. Then there was the gigantic shining contraption, with a slow conveyor moving through it, that processed the cans and sealed the lids on them.

Out from the far end of this magic machine emerged shining silvery tin cans filled with our own produce. They were real cans just like the ones that you could buy in the grocery store—but there were no labels on them!

In order to identify the contents, there was a rack of rubber stamps at the far end of the cooling rack. There were inked pads also. The rubber stamps spelled out every possible thing that could be preserved by canning. In alphabetical order, they started out, *Apples, Beans, Carrots*, all the way to *Zucchini*!

I loved to go to the cannery with Mama when she went to can our produce. Often, she and her sister Eddie would go and work together. I loved the smells and sounds of the place. I loved the heat produced by the steam pipes than ran everywhere and made it all work.

I turned eight years old the summer the cannery was first open. My little brother, Joe, was almost six. When both of us went to the cannery with Mama, she was terrified that Joe would get "scalded to death on the steam." So I had to take him outside so he would not get burned. I had never seen a child get scalded to death on steam, so I actually was curious about what that might look like!

My favorite thing about the cannery was the set of rubber stamps used to identify what had been canned. Mama would let me stamp the lids of the cans when they cooled down from the processor. I actually got to stamp each lid twice: once with the contents of the can and again with the date stamp that told when we had put up that run of produce. Joe would beg to help, but we all thought that he was too little to make the letters come out readable and even.

All through that summer, we canned stuff and canned stuff. There was one day when Mama got Daddy to kill and dress a dozen chickens at one time. Then she took all of the chickens over to the cannery. She and Aunt Eddie cooked them in one of the big steam cookers. Then, when the chickens cooled down, they took off all of the meat and discarded the skin and bones. After that, clean and fresh chicken meat was canned!

Another day, late in the fall of the year when hogs were killed, they canned pork and sausages. We were to be in food heaven when winter came.

It was a day in October when Daddy came home in the afternoon to make an announcement. "Lucille, I was listening to the radio in the car on the way home. There is going to be our first killing frost tonight. If there is anything left in the garden that you want to save, you better go out there and get it in before dark. It will all be gone in the morning."

Supper was delayed as Mama immediately coopted all of us to help, as she said, "strip the garden before the frost comes." We gathered all of the tomatoes left on the vines, both ripe and green. The green ones would be wrapped in newspaper and put in a cool place, where they would slowly ripen on into the fall. Daddy picked the last of the green beans. Mama cut the remaining okra. Joe and I were sent to pull remaining ears of corn from the sweet corn patch. There was a smattering of lima beans also. The onions could have stayed in the ground, but Mama pulled up a good dozen of them before we were finished. I knew she had something in mind.

I thought we were finished when Mama headed back out to the garden one last time.

"Aren't we finished?" Daddy asked.

"No!" she replied. "Let's pick up all of the apples that have fallen on the ground already. I have a plan for them."

Once back in the house, we all wanted to know what the plan was. Mama explained it while we sat at the table having our delayed supper.

"The cannery is still open on Saturdays," she started. "It won't close down for the winter until everyone has quit coming to put up things. So, this Saturday, I am going to go over there with everything that we have just gathered tonight and put it all together and make soup mix. Then, when we are cold and hungry in the wintertime, we can just open a can, maybe add some meat and potatoes, and have good soup for supper."

"Hah!" Daddy snorted. "I've never seen soup that had apples in it!"

"Not the apples, silly," Mama chuckled back at him. "I am going to use the apples to make a little run of my good, spiced applesauce. There's just enough to do that."

Now, we had all heard about her "good, spiced applesauce" for years, but no one in the family had ever tasted it. No, it was too good for us to eat—it had to be given away! Whenever we had applesauce, it was her plain, old flavorless applesauce that didn't have a grain of sugar to a gallon of it. That was simply the way it was.

Saturday came. Joe and I helped Mama take everything to the car. By now, all of the vegetables were washed and even trimmed a bit. It would be a good and productive day.

As soon as we got to the cannery, she said to me, "I do not want your little brother to get scalded to death on the steam. So, while I am working to put up this food, you take him outside and keep both of you out of trouble! I don't think it will take a long time because I don't really have a great deal of stuff to work with today. But I do have to do separate runs for the soup mix and the applesauce."

Reluctantly, I took Joe outside and started my job of resentful babysitting.

Behind the cannery building, there was a gravel road that went up the hill to the county school-bus garage. Beside the gravel road was an old pond. Anyone who looked at that pond could immediately tell that it badly needed to have rocks thrown into it. And since the little road was made of gravel, there were plenty of rocks ready for throwing. So Joe and I began to try to put those two things together the way they needed to be. We threw and chunked and tossed and skipped dozens of rocks.

We were having so much fun that it seemed as if no time had passed until Mama came to the back door of the cannery building and called to us, "Boys, where are you? Donald, I am ready for your help. Joe, you just stay right out there where you are and don't go anywhere."

She went on to me, "I have just filled up all of the cans and sent the soup mix into the processor. In a few minutes, those cans will come out the far end and be ready to have *Soup Mix* stamped on their lids. Right now, I'm getting ready to cut up the apples and cook them for the run of applesauce. In a few minutes, I want you to come on in here and stamp the soup mix while I am working on the applesauce."

Joe and I kept on throwing rocks. Something inside of me knew that the finished cans and the rubber stamps were at the far end of the building from where she was working, and that she would not know when or whether I had come in to do what she had asked. It was, at the time, more important to see how many rocks we could throw than to stamp the lids of the soup mix.

Time seemed to stand still as Joe and I continued to throw more and more rocks into the pond. I was totally surprised when Mama came to the back door of the cannery once again. This time, she started, "I have finished making the spiced applesauce.

The cans are going through the processor. They will be ready to stamp in a few minutes. Did you stamp the soup mix?"

I knew my mother. I knew the kinds of things that she liked to hear and the kinds of things that caused her personal concern and upset. I knew very well what she did not want to hear after asking that question. She did not want to hear me, her older child, say, "No, Mama. I deliberately chose to ignore what you asked me to do and to waste another hour of my life throwing rocks in a stagnant pond." I knew that those words would not make her happy.

So, for her benefit and her benefit alone, I said, "Yes, ma'am. I did it," because I knew that was the answer that would make her happy.

She said, "Oh, good. Then you can come on inside in a minute and stamp the lids on the applesauce while I clean everything up from all the mess I have made. Bring your little brother in with you 'cause we will go home after that."

With that, I turned to my brother, Joe, and said, "Come on, you are going to have to help me!" We headed inside.

We were at the far end of the cannery building from where Mama was washing pots and knives. She could not really tell from there what we were doing. I looked at all of the cans that had bunched up at the end of the conveyor belt upon coming out of the processor. Every one of them looked exactly like every other one, and there was no possible way in this world to tell what was actually inside any one of them.

I turned to Joe and said, "You are going to have to help me."

He smiled.

We hunted out the two stamps we were looking for from the rack on the wall. I held the one that said *Applesauce* and gave Joe the one that said *Soup Mix*. "Let's get busy," I ordered. "Half of them are applesauce, and half of them are soup mix."

We started stamping side by side. Every other can was *Applesauce*, and the ones in between were now marked *Soup Mix*.

As soon as we finished, we walked down the length of the cannery building to where Mama was just completing the cleanup. "We're through!" I announced.

"Oh, good," she replied.

Together, we loaded the cans of soup mix into one box and the cans of applesauce into another box and hauled them out to the car. At home, we took the cans down into the small basement space under the back porch where all the canned goods were kept through the winter. And everything was fine—until about December.

Every Sunday, we went to Sunday school and church at the Methodist church in town. I had learned from observation why Daddy loved to go to church so much. First of all, he loved to sing, and at church we sang old, familiar hymns and spiritual songs every week. But there was another reason. After the opening hymn, Daddy would settle down in the pew. For the rest of the service, his lower jaw would not move. But gradually, especially once the sermon started, his eyes would droop, then close, and his head would tilt back, back, back until his mouth was wide open.

That's when the snoring started. It was not loud, just regular and pleasant heavy breathing. Mama knew better than to touch him once he arrived at this state. If she so much as touched him, he would jerk wide awake, shaking the entire pew, and snort, "I'm not asleep, I'm just resting my eyes," in a voice you could hear all over church. After that happened once, he could sleep peacefully in church every Sunday, and she left him alone. Daddy would wake up when the last hymn started and sing all the way through it. Then came the benediction and time to go home.

There were three perfectly good escape routes out of that church. But instead of going out of one of the side doors, we had to get in line and go out the main door, where we had to shake hands with the preacher. The family would be in line—Daddy in the front, Mama next, then Joe and me in back.

Daddy would get to our preacher first, stick out his hand, shake the preacher's hand, and say, "That was fine this morning!" I knew what he was talking about. It was not the sermon but rather his nap that was fine! Then, without pause, the following invitation always came: "How about you-all coming home to eat dinner with us?"

Mama would be right behind him in the line. I could see her

reaction to the instant invitation. She would be shaking her head, frowning, looking at the preacher like she was going to stare a hole through him. It was a look of absolute panic.

Our minister was good at reading nonverbal language. He would wink at Mama and say to Daddy, "Thank you, Joe, but we've already got plans for today. I appreciate the invitation all the same."

December came. When the first Sunday of the month rolled around, we were off to church as usual. When we got there, we had a visiting minister—probably the Methodist district superintendent.

The service started. We sang Christmas songs, even though I knew that it was only Advent. Then I watched Daddy settle down for his Sunday-morning nap. It was going to be a good, long one today, as the visiting minister did not care how long he kept us, since he did not have to live with our congregation once he was gone.

Finally, the long pre-Christmas sermon ended, we sang the closing hymn, and it was time to go home.

"Let's just slip out the side, Joe. It's late!" I heard Mama say. I already knew this was a pointless suggestion.

"No, Lucille. We have to tell him how much we enjoyed having him here."

We all dutifully fell into line. It moved slowly today, as the visiting minister had to meet and converse a little bit with every single person in line. At last, it was our family's turn.

"That sure was fine!" Daddy was already laying out the compliment as he stuck out his hand. "I'm Joe Davis. Why don't you come home and have dinner with us?"

It all happened so quickly that Mama didn't even have time to react. Besides, that visiting minister had no idea who the woman was who was starting to have a fit in the line. By then, he had already answered, "Oh, how nice. We would love to!"

Until that moment, none of us knew that there was a "we" to it. Soon, we were to learn that he had a hungry wife and three underfed children waiting in the back pew.

The trip home in the car was very interesting. I thought that Mama had stepped on a nail after missing her tetanus shot. Her jaws were clamped tightly together as she talked hotly through her teeth. Her eyes were burning the air toward Daddy. "What in the world were you thinking of?" Her teeth were clenched. "We do not have one single thing in that house that is ready to feed someone, let alone that preacher. We are going to be the most embarrassed people on the face of the earth. I do not understand what in this wide world you were thinking about when you invited them to come home to dinner with us!"

About that time, my brother, Joe, popped up over the backseat with an observation: "It did Mama a lot of good to go to church today, didn't it?"

Daddy didn't dare laugh!

Finally, there was a chance for him to say a word. "Oh, Lucille. This is just the thing that you have been waiting for. It is what you spent all summer getting ready for. I tell you what I was thinking of. I was thinking about all of the good stuff that you put up at the cannery all this year. Here's what to do: Get a can of that good chicken meat, and you can whip up some chicken and dumplins in a minute. Get a can of green beans and a can of beets. You will have Sunday dinner on the table before they find their way to our house. It will be easy!"

There was no time to argue. By the time we pulled into our driveway at home, the orders had been lined out. I was sent to hurry to the basement and get two cans of chicken and then come back to help in the kitchen. Joe started out on two trips for double cans of green beans and beets. Daddy was instructed to get the white tablecloth and set the table with the good dishes and silverware.

Water was boiled and tea was made. Dumplins were rolled out and went into the pot with chicken and gravy. Beets were heated with the juice thickened and sweetened. Green beans had fatback added and boiled away, though Mama was certain that they would not have time to get seasoned enough to taste good.

Sure enough, by the time the guest preacher and his family got to our house, the food was ready to put on the table.

After extended greetings, fanciful compliments, and a long blessing, it was all served. The meal was wonderful. With the dumplins, there was no need for bread. All was complete. We all had as much as anyone could expect from a full Sunday dinner. Everyone was satisfied—except Daddy.

"Well, that was good, Lucille. What's for dessert?"

I was about eight years old when this happened, and as far as I could remember we had not had dessert for at least twenty-five years.

Mama looked like she had swallowed a frog. She was afraid to look at Daddy, lest her look itself kill him. She stumbled and stuttered, then recovered. "This is the perfect time to have some of my good, spiced applesauce," she said. "Donald, go on down to the basement and bring us a can, please."

I headed to the basement and returned with the properly stamped can of applesauce. Mama got the can opener and started on the can.

As soon as the can opener broke through the lid, as soon as Mama began to turn the little handle to cut the can open, you could tell that something did not smell right. There was a food odor, but it was not the smell of spice or applesauce. Mama lifted the severed lid from the can, and there it was—a full can of soup mix.

"There has been a mistake," she said to me. "You must not have seen it well in the dark. Run back down there, and be sure that this one says *Applesauce.*"

I was on the way and careful to carry out the order correctly. Soon, the second can marked *Applesauce* rested on the kitchen counter.

Mama opened it. It was another can of soup mix.

"Quick," she said, "run and get another one."

She opened six cans of soup mix in a row before she gasped,

"Go get one this time that says *Soup Mix.*"

We finally had applesauce!

At last, the visiting minister, his well-filled wife, and the three children went home.

We had vegetable soup for six nights in a row until things finally got back to normal at our house.

The next Sunday, I was watching Daddy carefully to see what would happen when we went to church. As usual, he slept through the sermon with our regular minister back in the pulpit. When it was over, we lined up to go out the door and speak to the preacher. Mama was right behind Daddy. She had a hold on his coattail with both hands at the same time.

Daddy approached the minister. "That was fine!" came the usual compliment. At that moment, I saw Mama give his coattail a terrific yank. Daddy stood up very straight and continued to our minister, "And we'll see you next Sunday!"

Never again did he invite anyone to have dinner at our house without personally applying to Mama at least two weeks ahead of time. And I had learned something about marriage way before I needed to.

Straight to Heaven?

From the time of earliest memory, we went to the Methodist church in Waynesville every, every, every, every Sunday.

But I never gave up! We would get up on Sunday morning and sit down at the table for breakfast. I would look across the table at my daddy and ask, "What are we going to do today?"

He would shyly smile and always answer the same way: "Don't you know what day this is?"

I was ready. "Yes. It's Sunday. There is no school today, so I was wondering what we are planning to do today."

"We're going to church."

"We went last Sunday."

He took the bait, as always. "Well, we are going to go again. You know, if we are not there, they won't really have church."

"Then let's stay home and give everybody a break." This was my last effort.

It did not work. We indeed did go to church every Sunday.

Sunday mornings always rolled out in the same way. On Sunday only, Mama would fix pancakes for breakfast. I can still see the Log Cabin syrup can shaped like a small, tin log cabin, with its chimney being the pouring spout, sitting in a shallow hot-water bath on the stove before it came with the first batch of pancakes to the table.

We would eat our breakfast together, then Joe and I would take our baths and get ready for church while Mama cooked our Sunday dinner. Her goal was to have our dinner completely fixed before we left for Sunday school. Then it could be stored in the refrigerator, and when we got home (after two or three semesters at church), all we had to do was warm it up and eat.

Once everyone was ready, we would all pile into the Plymouth, and Daddy would drive us into town to First Methodist Church. Ours was usually one of the first two or three cars to arrive, so we always got to park on Academy Street right next to the door that went into our Sunday-school classrooms.

The first hour at church was not bad. It was, after all, Sunday school. We went to age-level rooms, sang "Jesus Loves Me," put a dime into the aluminum offering plate, drank some juice, said a Bible verse, then got to play for the rest of the hour. I was dismayed when I got to the fourth-grade class and learned that there were no toys in Sunday school past the first-to-third-grade class.

After that first hour, we would get out of Sunday school when a bell rang. Joe and I would find one another, and we would try to decide whose turn it was to ask the all-important question for this week: "Do we have to stay for big church?"

No matter how many times we asked it, there was always only one answer: "Yes!"

Then Mama would take over. "You boys go to the bathroom."

Joe and I would answer in unison, "We don't need to go to the bathroom."

"Go anyway."

"We just went on the way up here from Sunday school."

"Go again."

"I can't go!"

"Try!"

Then, even though we knew there would be a dry outcome, we would each go and try. This was because we were allowed to do only two things in church: "Be-have!" For our mother, behavior did not include leaving church to go to the bathroom. We knew that we could float out of big church on Noah's second flood and we would still never be excused to leave the sanctuary in the middle of the service to go to the bathroom.

I go to church these days and watch the children wear trails in the carpet running back and forth, back and forth to the bathroom. I look at them and wonder, *Where are their parents?* As a Methodist, I have never thought a lot about the Rapture, but if it does come I hope that it is during church when all those children are out in the bathroom. Just imagine their all coming back from another unnecessary trip and everyone in church is *gone.* They missed the whole thing because they were out there in the bathroom when Jesus came back to get them.

After the useless bathroom trip ordeal, we could climb the big stairs up to the sanctuary level and head in through the vestibule toward *our* seats. Somewhere, there is a lost chapter in the book of Genesis in which Adam (after naming the animals) assigned everyone in perpetuity their seats in church. You know good and well that if you go to church and sit in the wrong seat, you do not even get credit for it. The credit probably goes to the person whose seat you took to begin with.

In that lost ancient chapter, our family was assigned the fourth pew from the front on the right-hand side of First Methodist Church. Our pew was right beside the stained-glass window that had the dead Atkins family's names in it. To this day, I can still tell you that Bishop James Atkins was born April 18, 1850, and died December 5, 1923, because I read that on the window every Sunday.

Our family always entered our pew in the same order. My little brother, Joe, would go in first. (Our parents wanted to keep us as

At our "new" house on the way to church when I was about twelve

far apart as possible.) My father entered next. He sat beside Joe with his left hand resting on Joe's right knee. Having been born in 1901, Daddy was too old to be in World War II. So, for his wartime home-defense duty, he took Red Cross training and taught Red Cross first-aid classes. This meant that he well knew every pressure point in the human body. So, with his hand on Joe's knee, if that little child did anything even slightly untoward, Daddy could vise down on his knee and Joe would limp for about two weeks.

Next, Mama entered the pew. She would sit next to Daddy, and he would put his arm around her, resting it on the back of the wooden pew like he loved her. Mostly, though, this was so that his right-hand grasp was ready for my shoulder when I came in to my regular place on the end of the pew. I liked to sit next to the aisle and hang my arm over the end of the pew like I was grown up.

There was no air conditioning in the church in those days. It was not because air conditioning had not been invented. No, it was because everyone knew that air conditioning would have made it far too comfortable in church, and that would have spoiled part of the reason for being there. So, when it got too hot as the morning progressed, one of the ushers would quietly slip down the side aisle and pull a little chain on each of the tall stained-glass windows. The chain opened and rotated a section of the window, top and bottom, and the breeze could now flow freely through the sanctuary.

I was about eight years old when, one autumn Sunday, the sanctuary heated up and Hardy Noland, who was ushering that day, eased down the aisle and opened our window. Little did we know that outside that window, waiting for just this moment, was a very large and very heathen yellow jacket. As soon as the window opened, the yellow jacket took flight. It silently drifted in the window, looking specifically for me. I was, of course, paying total attention to the sermon and did not see it coming. That ill-mannered creature landed on the crook of my right-hand little finger, cocked its stinger, and simply stung the Methodist out of me.

Very slowly and silently, I turned to my mother and held my ill-treated finger up in front for her to see.

She took one glance at the poor finger, glared at me, and said, "Ssshhh!"

I hadn't even said anything! Thinking that she did not see it or she would not have reacted this way, I held it closer up to her face and whispered, "I got stung!"

"Ssshhh!" came her reply.

"It hurts!"

"Ssshhh!"

"I need to go out."

This was too much for her. Through clenched teeth, she gave

me a loud stage whisper: "Be quiet. I am trying to listen to the sermon!"

I had to sit there on the very edge of death for the rest of that entire hour, watching my finger change colors and swell up to about three times the size it was meant to be.

Finally, church was over, and we headed home.

"I got stung by a yellow jacket!" I reported it again, just in case she still didn't get it.

"I know that," she started. "That's why you were trying to make such a fuss in church."

"It hurt. I needed to go out!"

"It would have hurt just as much outside as it hurt if you stayed in there," was her reply. "Besides, you know that we do not leave church for frivolous reasons."

"It was not frivolous. If I had been allergic, I could have *died!*"

She was calm in her response. "That would have been fine. If you had died in church, you might have gone straight to heaven. And that, mister, might be your only chance!"

"I don't think it works that way," I wailed.

But it made no difference. The entire totality of first-aid treatment I got for the sting was a little dab of spit on Mama's finger, dipped into the baking-soda box and then touched to my finger.

Nothing was going to change. I think that was when I knew why no one else sat on the same pew with our family. It was being reserved for our eventual wives and children. I was never going to get out of that place.

The years passed. By the time I was about eleven or twelve years old, I made a wonderful discovery. In our church sanctuary, there was a big upstairs balcony across the back. My discovery, as it was explained to me by several older boys, was that when you became thirteen years old, you got to go upstairs, away from your family, and sit in the balcony with all the other boys who were thirteen and older. On Sundays, I noticed that this seemed to be true. So I began to count the weeks until I could join that special club.

Finally, my thirteenth birthday arrived. There was a slight

marking of my birthday during the week of its passing, and then Sunday arrived. We were moving through the vestibule when I headed toward the balcony stairs.

Mama spoke to me: "Where are you going?"

"I am going up to the balcony." Couldn't she see this without my having to tell her?

"There's not time for you to go up there and back before church starts."

"I'm not going up there and back. I'm just going up there."

"What for?" She looked honestly puzzled.

"I am now thirteen years old, and in this church when you are thirteen you get to go sit up in the balcony with the other mature young men."

She didn't even argue. She just smiled and shook her head. "Un-uh. We sit on the fourth row downstairs. We do not sit in the balcony."

I did argue. "Not fair. When you are a thirteen-year-old boy, you get to sit in the balcony. All of the other boys told me that. Only girls keep sitting with their families after they are thirteen."

She smiled more this time. "I always wanted a girl. Now, let's go to our seats."

"This is not fair! Why do all the other boys get to sit upstairs and I don't get to?"

"That is why!" She began one of her nonsensical statements. "It is because all the other boys are up there that you cannot go up there. And besides, it has to do with horseplay. One Sunday, Eddie Weatherby and Joe Jennings got into horseplay during the offering. They knocked the offering plate off of the balcony. It came raining down, with money going everywhere. It hit Dr. Nick Medford in the top of the head, and you can still see the dent. That is why you cannot go sit upstairs."

"That has nothing to do with me," I pled.

"I think it does," was all she said.

That was the end of it. I was to be stuck downstairs with my family forever.

The year rolled along through the summer, through the fall, and into early December. We had gotten a new minister in June, Mr. Brendall. My daddy's nickname for him was "Old Push-up." Daddy had nicknames for all of our preachers, most of which are not to be publicly published.

There was a specific reason that he called this new preacher "Old Push-up." Mr. Brendall had heavy-lensed glasses and did not seem to see well. On top of that, he wrote out his sermons and then read them from the pulpit when the appropriate time came.

So sermon time would come, and Old Push-up would place the manuscript on the pulpit and reach up and grab the sides of the pulpit in push-up position. Then he would bend his elbows until his face was inches from the manuscript, read a little bit silently to himself, push up, and recite that line out loud to the congregation. It was down, up, down, up, over and over again until the entire sermon was read. Daddy said that Old Push-up certainly earned his name.

Well, there we were on that early-December morning when Old Push-up started in on the sermon. About that same time, the slight smell of something burning wafted up into our collective nostrils. I could see people glancing around at each other, but no one moved. Old Push-up either had a bad sense of smell or was so interested in his own sermon that he never noticed anything. He preached on.

The burning smell got stronger, and by then little wisps of smoke were coming up from the molding joint along the baseboard below the side-aisle windows. On the row in front of us sat the Hammetts, Frank and Doris, both doctors, and their three children. The smoke kept coming, and all of a sudden the Hammetts gathered up their children and left because they knew that they were essential!

Now, the white smoke was up to the window sills, and Mr. Brendall preached on. There was rustling behind us, and the Dulins got up and left, followed by the Medfords. Then, way on the other side of the church, the Massies got up and left, and there was not even any smoke over there. The sermon continued.

All of a sudden, my mother leaned down to me and quietly whispered, "Let's go!"

I looked straight at her and said, "Ssshhh!"

She looked at me like I didn't understand what she had said and spoke louder: "Something is on fire. Let's go!"

I, too, was louder: "Ssshhh!"

Now, she was not even whispering. "Get your stuff and let's go. Now!"

Since she didn't whisper, I didn't either. "Be quiet. I am trying to listen to the sermon!"

She turned away from me and gathered up my daddy and brother, Joe, and they climbed over me and went out of the smoky church, leaving me sitting there. I would not have moved if all that end of town was on fire. By the time the firemen got there, only Mr. Brendall and I were still in the smoke-filled sanctuary.

The source of the smoke was quickly located. Down under the sanctuary, in an old, superannuated Sunday-school room now being used as a storage room, someone had been pulling out all of the Christmas decorations. It was December cold in that basement room, and it had an old, open-flame gas heater in it from its Sunday-school days. The heater had been lighted and then not turned off when the decoration searchers left. They had left cardboard boxes too close to it, and there was a lot of smoldering and billows of smoke but not yet any actual flames.

Everything was fine—until we got in our car and started home.

"What in the world got into you?" It was between a hiss and a growl. "Why did you act like that? You embarrassed the life out of me. Why did you not leave when you were supposed to?"

"Because, Mama, you taught me that we do not just walk out of church for frivolous reasons!"

"This was not frivolous! There was a fire!"

"No, there was not a fire. It was just a lot of smoke. No one actually needed to leave at all." I smiled.

"Yes," she continued, "but if it had been a *real* fire, we could have all died!"

For a few moments, I just sat there looking at her and letting what she had said settle into the car. Then I was ready.

"That would have been *fine*. If we had all died in church, we might all have gone straight to heaven. And that might be our only chance!"

She was quick. "I don't think it works like that."

No more was said.

The following Sunday, we got up, ate pancakes, got dressed, and headed to church as always. As we passed into the vestibule, no words were spoken. Daddy just tapped me on the shoulder and pointed to the balcony stairs. I went up, and they stayed down.

From then on, Sunday was a much more pleasant day.

Miss Metcalf and the Potatoes

At the beginning of the third grade, a crisis began. The *A* through *Gr* group was assigned to a new and totally unknown teacher! Her name was Miss Ruth Metcalf, and my mama was in a panic. Not only was Miss Metcalf not from Haywood County, she was just out of college and had never taught school before, and I was to be in her class.

Mama went into action. She met Miss Metcalf and let her know that she, Mama, had started her teaching career as a third-grade teacher, so she knew everything there was to know about teaching third grade. She offered to be of any help to Miss Metcalf that might be needed, so that she would have a successful time with the *A*s through the *Gr*s—which mainly meant with me.

At first, I resented this interference. Later, however, I came to appreciate Mama's actions. What I gradually realized was that Mama's attention somehow turned me into Miss Metcalf's pet student. After all, I knew all there was to know about Hazelwood School, and I could be a lot of help to a new and inexperienced teacher! I knew where to find things that she needed. I knew all of the other teachers plus Haskell Davis, the janitor, and Mrs. Calhoun, the lunchroom lady, so I could run errands of every kind for Miss Metcalf if she needed things done. It turned out that I had a very special position. I was almost the informal teacher's aide in my own third-grade classroom.

It was easy to get Miss Metcalf off the subject and into storytelling. We were good at it! When we asked questions, she actually thought we were interested, and she would go into great detail to satisfy our curiosity.

Two things always worked. We discovered early on that her father had been a Japanese prisoner of war in World War II. There was no end to the speculative questions we learned to ask about him, and no end to her appreciation of our interest in her own family stories. She told us again and again about the Bataan Death March and about the abstruse and creative ways prisoners learned to live, eat, and survive during the course of their captivity. She told us that her father was determined not to lose his class ring while he was a prisoner of war, and that he often hid it in his mouth or in the soap so it would not be taken from him.

The other thing we learned was that she had a very serious boyfriend. Actually, at the end of the year, we learned that Miss Metcalf was not coming back to teach at Hazelwood School a second year because she was going to get married and would be moving away from Haywood County. The gradual movement through the year from boyfriend to fiancé gave us enough curiosity information to distract her from arithmetic for days and days.

It was on a bright winter day when Miss Metcalf called me up to her desk. I knew from the look on her face that she was about to send me on an errand! I was ready.

She had a very red face and nose and had been sniffling, blowing, wiping, and sneezing all day. She needed help.

Up beside her desk where she could talk privately with me, she started: "I have a terrible cold. It is all in my head, and I can hardly breathe. Some of the teachers have been talking about a new kind of nose drops. They are called Neo-Synephrine, and I am pretty sure that they have them at the Hazelwood Pharmacy." She opened her pocketbook and pulled out some money. "It won't take long, but do you think you would mind going down to the Hazelwood Pharmacy and seeing if Doc Keenum could send me some of those new nose drops? If they are as good as people say, it might save the whole day!"

I was as excited as I could be! I had heard about Mr. Hannah, one of the teachers, actually sending David Whitener to the drugstore to get him some Life Savers when he had a cough, but I had never been sent on an errand all the way into town to the drugstore. This would be a new adventure for sure.

Miss Metcalf gave me a five-dollar bill. There would be some change. I got my jacket and cap from the cloakroom. It was a sunny day but still was on the edge of winter. She wished me good luck and told me to get a box of Kleenex if there was enough money left over. That was all the money she had. I was off.

In ordinary measurement, it was the equivalent of a little more than two blocks to the Hazelwood Pharmacy. The short way, however, was to cut across the playground instead of following the sidewalk all the way around the Baptist church.

I jumped the tiny creek that ran through the playground and angled across past the Boy Scout building to where I could easily intersect Main Street. By the time I would get to Main Street going this way, I would be nearly halfway there.

Just off the back edge of the school playground, still not quite all the way to Main Street, there was a little store that was positioned there for no reason other than that all the kids who walked would pass it twice a day on their way to and from school. To call it a "store" was perhaps a stretch, though we all called it that. It was in reality the body of a superannuated school bus. The engine end was gone, and the rest of the bus was painted bright red. It was permanently and tirelessly mounted on concrete blocks with a set of two concrete-block steps leading to the old bus door. The man who owned and ran the little store seemed always to be sit-

Daddy when he married Mama

ting sideways on the old driver's seat, where he watched the door and was ready to pull the handle to open it whenever anyone walked up.

The little red bus store had fascinated me ever since I entered the first grade at Hazelwood School. You could look off to the side and see it as you rode in a car up Main Street to turn on Virginia Avenue to go to school. From school, you could look across the playground and never miss its shining and inviting red color calling you toward it.

I had never been in this small, magical place. Mama strictly prohibited it, even though we never passed there with a chance to enter anyway. She called it "a money-sucking place." "That little red bus," she would frown. "That little red bus is an evil place. It will suck the lunch money right out of the pockets of hungry and unfed children. They ought to find a way to push that thing over and fill dirt in over the top of it!"

How much more fascinating could it be?

So, on this special errand day, I was forced to walk exactly past the little red school-bus store on my way to the Hazelwood Pharmacy. My hands were in my pockets, so I could easily feel the nickel and dime that I had there, left from some kind of shopping trip or another. It was my money. My lunch was already paid for for the entire week. If I went in that store, it could not possibly suck the lunch money out of my pocket. It was safe for me to enter!

The little, dried-up, grouchy store man saw me coming. As soon as my foot neared the bottom step of the door, he pulled the handle and opened his world to me. "Come right in!" he coughed. "Have yourself a look around. I don't think I remember seeing you in here before, but you must go to Hazelwood."

"I don't usually walk to school," was my answer. "Now, I'm on an official errand, and I need to get warm."

I was already looking all over the little bus at the treasures that were offered there. Right beside the door, where the front seats of the old bus had been removed, there was a cold-water soft-drink box. I knew that if I lifted the lid it would be filled with Coca-Colas and Pepsi-Colas and Dr Peppers and Tru-Ades and Nehis and all kinds of other bottled soft drinks. This was not for me.

Across from the cold-drink box and just behind the man in his driver's seat, there was an installed gas heater with its blue flame growling. This was how he kept warm in here all day long, even through the coldest days of the winter. I was fascinated.

There were wooden shelves all along the sides of the old bus, right up to the level of the windows. One side had a few legitimate groceries—bread and crackers and some cans of Campbell's

Soup. There was even a small refrigerator that I guessed had milk in it, even though I was afraid to open the door and look.

The real treasure was all along under the windows on the street side. Next to the cold-drink box was an ice-cream freezer with its square-knobbed lids. It was covered with pictures of Nutty Buddies and Brown Mules and Creamsicles. Beyond it came shelves and shelves of nothing but pure candy! There were peanut butter logs and Baby Ruths. There were Hershey bars (with and without nuts!) and Mars bars and Clark bars and Butterfingers. There were Coconut Slices with three colors of coconut. There were Necco Wafers and peppermint sticks and every variety of chewing gum and bubble gum you could possibly think of in the world.

I hardly noticed that there were cigarettes and cigars and pipe tobacco beyond the candy, as the candy was the total focus of my too-long attention.

What to get? What to get? The *whether* question had never come up in my mind. I was there with money and no mother to stop me. Of course I was going to get something.

The little, dried-up store man was watching my every move like I was a shoplifter from *Oliver Twist*. He finally commented, "Yer gonna wear it out from looking before you ever taste anything if you don't make up yer mind."

I was working on it.

Suddenly, the decision was made. I picked up a little pack of five tiny paraffin bottles called Nik-L-Nips. They were in a miniature cardboard carrying case, and they looked like tiny Coca-Cola bottles. Each of the five Nik-L-Nips was filled with a different colored liquid. They cost—guess what?—a nickel!

The little, dried-up man didn't look very happy that that was all I was buying, but he did not hesitate to take my money. I headed out the door of the little store with the Nik-L-Nips and could not wait to get into them.

As soon as I got to Main Street and turned the corner, there was a green wooden bench beside the street. I sat down on the bench and proceeded to slowly drink the contents of all five

Nik-L-Nip bottles without stopping. I wanted to keep the little, empty paraffin bottles, but there was too much danger that Mama would find them in my pockets later. So, much to my sadness, I tossed them in the nearby trash can and headed on toward the Hazelwood Pharmacy.

In all of this, it never occurred to me that time was passing back in Miss Metcalf's room, or that she might be mentally calculating how long it ought to take for a third-grade boy to go on an errand to the drugstore and back. As far as I was concerned, I was on important business, and time had nothing to do with it.

I knew the Hazelwood Pharmacy very well. It was our family and town drugstore. The place was owned and run by Doc Keenum, a tiny bald man whom everyone of every age felt free to call "Little Doc." I pushed open the door of the store and went inside. The lunch counter was on the left side, and the pharmacy was in the back on the right of the small store. I headed straight for the pharmacy. This was important!

Little Doc stopped what he was doing to look down at a child out of school in his store. "What are you doing here, little Davis?"

I handed him the paper on which Miss Metcalf had written "Neo-Synephrine nose drops" and explained it. "My teacher has a bad cold. She sent me down here to get her some of these new nose drops to help her out with it. I guess you know what they are?"

"I know what they are, all right. So does everybody else in this town. I am flat sold out until the new order comes on Friday. She is going to have to suffer until then." He handed the paper back to me and turned back to what he had been doing.

I was struck at the same time by a feeling of disappointment and another awareness: I had been gone too long to return empty-handed. This much time would not be noticed if I returned with the nose drops, but I had been gone too long to go back with nothing.

That's when the idea showed up all on its own. I knew that Smith's Drug Store in Waynesville was a lot bigger than Little Doc Keenum's store, and it would surely have the nose drops!

Hazelwood and Waynesville were in reality two little towns that ran together. Today, Hazelwood has been merged into Waynesville and no longer has a separate incorporation. But then, if you went up Main Street in Hazelwood, just past the turn back to school, you intersected with Main Street of Waynesville. If you turned left on this different Main Street, in less than a mile you would be in the middle of the larger of the two towns and right in front of Smith's Drug Store.

I also knew that there was a shorter way to get there. If you crossed the street and headed straight up toward LeRoy Roberson's house, you were on a shortcut route toward Waynesville. It seemed to me that I could go that way and then intersect with the route to Waynesville, and it would be a lot shorter. Besides, even if it took some time, it would be better to take the time and come back with the nose drops than simply to give up and return to Miss Metcalf empty-handed.

I started out. My route took me over by the Presbyterian church, up the hill past Chuck Border's, and then toward LeRoy's. I cut through the woods and ended up coming out near the Stackpoles' house, then went down the sidewalk by the Watkinses' house, and I was at least halfway to my goal. I knew exactly where I was and was feeling so smart and clever to have solved the problem all on my own.

My route continued past the Dulins' house, past Clyde Ray's Flower Shop, past Ernie Crawford's Gulf station, past the Baptist church, and on into the middle of town. I pushed open the door of Smith's Drug Store and headed back to the pharmacy.

"I am on a special errand for my teacher." Somehow, it seemed like my presence there during school warranted some explanation. "She is sick and needs this."

I handed the druggist the note that had "Neo-Synephrine nose drops" printed on it. He took the note, turned around, went to the right shelf, and returned with a small bottle of nose drops. Success! There was enough change left to buy her the box of Kleenex she also hoped for. I felt big all over.

Now, all I had to do was get back to Hazelwood School. The shortcut way I had come seemed surely to be the best way back. It was back up Main Street and then through a couple of yards and over the hill back toward LeRoy's house.

About the time I got to the top of the wooded hill, I heard a sound of great interest. It was the wail of a siren.

Of course, I stopped and tried to see where the sound was coming from. Down through the trees, I could still see Main Street. As the sound grew louder, I could see Waynesville's black Plymouth police car moving very fast with the red light on top blinking as the siren wailed. No fire truck followed. I figured it must be some kind of robbery or something to bring about such a response. The car went on out of sight, and I headed on into the woods and over the top of the hill. At about that time, I heard the siren again, but this time the sound came from over in Hazelwood. From here, I could see all the way down into the middle of town. That's when I saw that it was not the same siren. The one Hazelwood police car, a black and white Ford, was headed up Main Street with its own siren wailing away. I figured this must be something bad, but I kept on going.

As I came down the hill past LeRoy Roberson's house and got closer to Hazelwood's Main Street, I could see that both police cars had turned up Virginia Avenue toward my school. I really wondered now what had happened while I was finishing the errand for Miss Metcalf. My pace picked up as I got closer. I was anxious to know what I had missed.

Going now up Virginia Avenue beside the Baptist church, I could see all the way up the street past the school, and what I saw was confusing in the least. There were both the Waynesville and Hazelwood police cars, there was a car that looked exactly like my daddy's car (even though I knew he was supposed to be at work at the bank), and there was a group of close to a dozen people in a kind of huddle.

As I got closer, I could identify the people: they were Mr. Leatherwood, our principal; Miss Metcalf, my teacher; my daddy; my mama; two policemen; and Mr. Stephens, the truant officer. Miss Metcalf and my mama both looked like they were crying. The men looked like they were serious. They were all looking at each other, and so they did not even see me coming.

I walked right up to the huddle before even being noticed, then I handed the paper bag to Miss Metcalf and said, "Here's your Neo-Synephrine, Miss Metcalf. It ought to make you feel better."

One of the policemen looked at me and said, "Is this the one?" All the adults together just nodded.

Then the policeman said what I thought to be a very strange thing: "Well, now that he's back, do you want to keep him?"

Of course they want to keep me, I thought. *Why, I just carried out a difficult errand when most other kids my age would have given up.* I was totally proud of myself.

Daddy hugged both Mama and Miss Metcalf and said to Mr. Leatherwood and the policemen together, "Everything's all right now. You can all go back to work. I'll just have a few words with Miss Metcalf."

This seemed to suit Mr. Leatherwood just fine. Better for my daddy to deal with things than that he should have to. They all walked away, leaving the four of us standing there.

"Everything really is all right," he said to Miss Metcalf. "But I would like for you to come over to our house this evening and have supper with us. I know that you don't have a car, so I shall pick you up about six o'clock."

She wiped her eyes and nodded her head, and we went back to class.

For the rest of that day, we did not have to try to do anything new in Miss Metcalf's class. She either read to us or let us have reading time on our own. I really thought that we could have done almost anything and, as long as we did it quietly, she would never have noticed.

That afternoon, Daddy seemed to come home from work a little earlier than usual. He even changed his clothes and offered to help Mama with supper. She didn't take him up on his offer.

A little before six, he asked me if I wanted to ride with him to go pick up Miss Metcalf. I did. We rode into town and to the boardinghouse on Pigeon Street where she lived with several other unmarried teachers.

When we knocked on the door, she came out dressed up like she was on her way to church, rather than supper. She turned down my offer to let her ride in the front with Daddy and got into the backseat, while I stayed in the front. There was no conversation on the way back to our house.

When we got home, Mama was not quite ready for us to sit down to eat. She asked me to show Miss Metcalf around where we lived, and she told me it was okay to take her outside. I did, and we went all around through the yard and then past the garden, the chicken house, and the barn. Miss Metcalf told me that she had grown up on a farm and that being at our house made her homesick.

In a little while, Mama called from the door for us to come in to supper. When we went inside, Mama had set the table in the dining room instead of the kitchen. This was not normal for a weeknight. Daddy directed all of us as to where to sit—this was not normal either—and I ended up on the side beside my teacher.

After the blessing, we dug in. Mama had fixed fried chicken with gravy, mashed potatoes, green beans, orange Jell-O with grated carrots mixed in, and her homemade yeast rolls. It felt like something between Sunday and Thanksgiving. Everyone ate and ate, and there was a little bit of visiting conversation that went on during the course of the meal. When we finished eating, everyone at the table looked relaxed and full.

Daddy pushed back in his chair and looked at Miss Metcalf. "We wanted to have you over tonight so you could know us a little better. I know that this is your first year teaching and that you are not from around here, so I thought it might help you some to know some of the parents you are dealing with, what we are like, and what we ourselves happen to like and dislike."

Miss Metcalf looked very serious now; it was like all of the good food's influence had just worn off.

Daddy went on, "So let me tell you a little story."

Oh, boy, I thought. *She really doesn't know what she's in for now.* I knew my daddy could come up with a story to teach a person about anything he thought they needed to know.

He started, "When I was a little boy, I grew up on a farm way out in the north end of Haywood County in the community of Iron Duff. I was number eight in a long run of thirteen children, and we had to work very hard just to raise enough each year to feed all of us. My daddy, Donald's granddaddy, was off in Raleigh in the legislature in the wintertime, and he wanted to be sure that he left Mama and all of us with enough to eat until he got back each year.

"Well, it was 1913, and I was twelve years old in February. That spring, we put in the biggest crop of Irish potatoes I could remember our ever having. Daddy said we could live off of potatoes if we ran out of everything else. When the end of the summer came and we dug all of the potatoes, even he was surprised. We had fifty-two bushels of potatoes to keep in the basement under the house, and we still had a full wagonload of those Irish potatoes left.

"Daddy had heard that there was a man with a railroad car on a siding over near Ed Fincher's store in Clyde who was set up there buying people's extra potatoes. He told me that he sure would like to take this wagonload of potatoes over there and sell them, but he just didn't have the time to spend a whole day doing that. Then he looked at me and asked me if I thought I was old enough to take the wagon with our team of horses over to Clyde and sell the potatoes for us."

He went on. I had never heard this story before, so it was very interesting to me.

"I had, and still have, a cripple leg. I cut it with an ax when I was five years old. I couldn't plow with horses because I couldn't manhandle the plow to turn it when plowing, but I could handle sitting up on the wagon and working from there with our two horses. As soon as I told him that I thought I could do it, he told me that tomorrow would be the day—if he could talk Mama into letting me go by then.

"I reckon he must have talked her into it because at supper he announced the plan to the whole family. My older brothers Moody and Harry said they knew I could do it. My younger brother, Frank, wanted to go and help, but Mama put a quick end to that idea. The plan was for me to leave right at daylight. That way, Daddy thought I could get to Clyde, sell the potatoes, and make it home before dark. I hardly slept at all that night because I had never done anything like this in my whole life.

"The next morning, Mama had a good breakfast for me and sent me with a big chunk of cornbread and a jug of sweet milk to get me through the day. Daddy hitched the horses up to the wagon, and I was on the way. It was a wonderful late-summer day. The air was crisp and had the tiniest feel of fall in it. I still remember that the birds were singing like they were having a great big party before cold weather began to come in.

"Well, here's what happened. I got over to Clyde and didn't see a train car on the siding anywhere. So I went in Ed Fincher's store and asked a man working in there about where the potato-buying man was to be found. That's when I ran into a little trouble. That man in the store told me that the potato man had left the afternoon before and had moved his train car over to Canton, where he was buying potatoes down near the paper mill. Canton was a good three or so miles away.

"So what was I going to do? Was I going to give up and go on back home and meet failure when everybody saw that I was sent to sell the potatoes and didn't do the job? Or was I going to go on to Canton, which I had not been told to do, and sell the potatoes there and be in trouble for going a place I had not been told to go? Either way seemed like a bad option. I thought about it while I ate the cornbread and milk, and then I decided.

"*If I am going to get in trouble*, I thought to myself, *it's better to get into trouble with the potatoes sold than with them not sold.* So I got back on the wagon and headed three more miles on over the hill and down into Canton.

"Way down at the end of one of the sidings at the Champion paper mill, I found the train car. The man had it about three-quarters full of potatoes, and he told me that one more day and he would be gone for good. I felt like I was lucky that I made it. He had two men who were working for him load the potatoes from our wagon into his train car. Then he looked at how much they had added to what he already had, and he paid me four silver dollars for the wagonload of potatoes. I was proud because I had made a success of a day that could have turned out ruined.

"Just as I was about to turn the horses around with the wagon and head back toward Iron Duff, a little sidewinder switch engine started coming down the siding, moving two flatcars loaded with pulpwood. I didn't get those horses halfway around when here came that little engine huffing and puffing and spitting steam. Those horses went crazy. They stood up on their hind legs and started to let down and run. Before they could get their front feet back on the ground, I pulled back on the reins and wrapped them as tightly as I could around a stanchion on the side of the wagon bed. Those horses now couldn't get their front feet back on the ground, and they danced around in a circle, reared up on their hind legs, until that little train had passed. Then I let them down, and we started back toward Iron Duff.

"That little trip to Canton from Clyde had added a good six miles to my trip for the day, and I might should have been almost back home by now and had not even started. Well, I got on the way, and it was clear very soon that I was going to get home even later that I had guessed. By the time I was passing the Davis Chapel Church, it was already so dark that if both the horses and I had not already known the way we would have been lost. By the time I passed Aunt Charity Chambers's house, her light was blown out and the house was dark like they were already asleep.

"As I turned down the road to our farm, I was one worried boy. I knew that Mama and Daddy would be worried and likely awful mad by now. I just didn't know what was in store for the rest of the evening.

"Just as I came around the last curve where I could see the house, it looked like there was a light burning in every room; it was all lit up for sure. Besides that, I could see somebody standing out in the yard holding a lantern as they looked up the road, waiting for me to show up. I knew it was my daddy.

"As soon as I got in the yard, I jumped down off of the wagon, and both Mama and Daddy ran and hugged me. All I could say was, 'I sold the potatoes.' Daddy said, 'Go put the horses up and we'll talk back in the house.' This sounded bad to me.

"I unhitched the horses and put them in the barn. I gave each of them a good currying because I was not really in a hurry to get back to the house and have to face the music. Finally, I couldn't hold out any longer, and I told the horses good night and walked from the barn back over to the house.

"Mama and Daddy were sitting and waiting for me in the kitchen. 'Well, son, seems like you had an extra long day. Why don't you tell us all about it.'

"Right then and there, I told the longest version I could tell of everything that had happened that day. I knew that the longer I could make the story last, the longer it would be for whatever punishment I was going to get to come. When I finished the whole story, I told again about how I got the four dollars for the potatoes and pulled the four silver dollars out of my overalls pocket and handed them to Daddy. He took the money in his hand, rolled the coins over and over, and looked at them.

"Then he looked straight at me. 'Joe,' he started slowly, 'it sounds to me like you had a very important day. It's a good day if only one important thing happens to us, and today you had two important things happen to you. First of all, you had to figure out something that you never had to figure out before. You had to make an original decision. And you did that. In the second place, you had a chance to learn something that you would never have learned any other way. That's pretty big for one day, and I think it is worth something.' He then took one of the four silver dollars and handed it to me. 'Keep this, Joe. It will remind you that this was an important day.' "

Daddy's story seemed now to be over, but he got up from his

chair and disappeared into his and Mother's bedroom. In just a minute, he came back out with something held in his hand. He handed it to Miss Metcalf. When she looked, we could all see that he had handed her a silver dollar.

"This was a good day, Miss Metcalf," he said. "You made a decision, and you learned something. That is always worth quite a lot. Now, Lucille, I believe we are ready for dessert."

Mama brought out her lemon meringue pie and began to serve it. When Miss Metcalf had two pieces, I knew that now everything was all right. My daddy had done it again.

The Little Weasel

Hazelwood Elementary School had, overall, a very stable year-to-year student and teacher population. We knew that almost all the same teachers were going to be there year after year; many had been teaching there since our parents had them as teachers. More than that, there were very few students who came or went. I cannot remember more than one student in any single year who either joined or left our class as the year progressed (not counting those who were occasionally graduated to the Stonewall Jackson Training School for the remainder of a certain year).

In Mrs. Annie Ledbetter's "*A* through *Gr*" first-grade class, there were twenty-eight of us. I can still name most of them, as this same group stayed together through elementary school. Most of them were still with me through my senior year in high school.

So a little boy named Luther Hooper was not in my room in

the first grade, since he was one of the *H*s. I knew who he was, though, from his playground and lunchroom reputation. Luther Hooper was a rusty-skinned boy who lived on Hyatt Creek. He always carried a knife to school (there was no rule against that), and he was known to challenge other boys to play the prohibited game of "Stretch" on the playground. (You stood facing your opponent, opened your knife, and threw it to stick in the ground as close as possible to the side of one of his feet. He had to move that foot out to where the knife stuck. It was then his turn to throw the knife close to your foot. This continued, alternating turns and alternating feet, until one person could "stretch" no more. What made it especially dangerous was that your turn didn't count if your knife did not stick in the ground or if it stuck more than a foot's width from the opponent's foot. This meant that there was real—and often bloody!—danger of a knife's being stuck in someone's foot.) Luther was also known to be seen smoking cigarettes in town on Saturdays. Besides that, I knew that he had been caught rolling dice in the hall before school in the mornings.

In the second grade, the "*A*s through the *Gr*s" all moved up together to old Miss Lois Harrell's class. That same year, my mama started back to teaching school, and she came to teach where I went to school at Hazelwood Elementary. I hated that! I had to ride to school with her in the morning and be seen getting out of the car with her. I had to hear her voice through the wall all day, as her classroom was next to Miss Lois Harrell's. And I had to be seen leaving school with her every afternoon.

In her return to teaching, she got the "*Gu*s through the *M*s" in her second-grade class. (I had lived all summer in fear that I would have to be one of her students.) This meant that Luther Hooper was in my mother's class for that year. What I learned from her was that he was "a bad boy" with whom I was not to associate if I knew what was good for me. I knew what was good for me, so I stayed far away from Luther Hooper.

I believe that it was not even during that year but the year after the second grade when Luther Hooper actually came to our house. He was not invited. It was a Sunday afternoon in the fall of the year, and our family had spent Saturday raking the leaves from the big red maples that shaded our front yard. I was out in the yard on Sunday, playing around the neat piles of leaves on what was a crisp, inviting autumn day.

All of a sudden, I heard a voice from the road in front of our house say, "Hey!" Plott Creek Road was still unpaved at this time, and there was very little traffic. And I had not heard the sound of a car anyway.

It was Luther Hooper riding an obviously recycled bicycle. The bicycle had a small wheel in front and a much larger wheel in the back. The frame had many signs of being welded together from parts and pieces, and it had not been repainted, so that the bicycle was red and blue with some green parts. The handlebars were very high, and as he rode Luther reached above his head to hold on to them. They looked like imaginary bull's horns.

Luther rode the strange bicycle right into our yard where I was playing. He rode it through the neat piles of leaves we had raked up the day before. He rode it straight toward a tree and at the last minute reared the bicycle up on its hind wheel, whipped it around on that one wheel, and came down headed away from the tree. It looked like a circus act to me, and I was very impressed with Luther.

He stopped the bicycle and got off near me. "You want to ride it?" he queried.

I did not even have a bicycle and had never ridden on one at all. I turned him down, but it seemed like I needed to say or ask something to counter his offer. "That's an interesting bicycle," I started. "I've never seen one like it. Where did you get it?"

"My uncle Charlie made it for me. It's got parts of six bicycles in it. That's why it's all of those different colors. The wheels even came off of two different bicycles that were different sizes."

"Why don't you paint it all the same color, like red all over?"

"Nah," he shot back quickly, "I'd rather have it like this. Besides, we ain't got no paint."

We were standing in the yard beside an upside-down two-wheel cart that Daddy called "the pushcart." He had brought it up from the barn the day before so we could load the leaves in it and haul them back to the garden, where they could be plowed in and rot before next year's gardening time.

Luther seemed very interested in the pushcart. He looked at it. "What do you call that thing? I've never seen anything like that."

"My daddy calls it a 'pushcart.' It's what we are going to haul the leaves in. He usually keeps it down at the barn, where he can use it to haul cow feed and stuff. He brought it up here yesterday."

Luther started spinning the wheels on the overturned cart. "These is good wheels, they are. If you was to want to make a go-cart, these would make awful good wheels for that." He spun them again.

At that moment, Mama came out the door onto the front porch. She marched over to the edge of the porch nearest us and folded her arms across her chest. "Luther!" She spoke sternly. "What are you doing all the way over here from Hyatt Creek? You go on back home. You don't need to be coming over here, and you know that. Get on that bicycle and go on now." Her voice was not mad, just stern. I could tell that she meant what she said.

Luther did not even answer her. He quickly picked up the hybrid bicycle, jumped on it, and took off. He was out of sight in half a minute.

Then she looked at me. "You better come on in the house in case he comes back. I don't think he will, but come in for a little while anyway. That boy knows he's not supposed to be over here."

"What's wrong with him, Mama?" I wanted to know.

"I don't guess anything is actually wrong with him. It's just that he hasn't had much raising. When he was in my room in the second grade, I never got anybody in his family to come to PTA all year long. They just don't take very good care of their children, and they don't know much themselves about right and wrong. I don't want you to play with him."

I knew that she didn't have to worry about that. As fascinating as it was to watch him do tricks on the bicycle, he was not anyone I wanted to get close to.

At the end of summer, it was time to go back to school. For three years, I had been in the "*A through Gr*" class grouping and had no reason to believe that this year was to be any different. It was a big surprise when, on the very first day in Miss Daisy Boyd's fourth grade, we discovered that this year our grouping had changed. The fourth-grade population must have shifted a bit from last year, and our new group was to be "*A through Ho.*" This meant that we were going to have our regular group (minus Johnny Duncan and Jansen Blanton, who had moved), plus Bobby Hannah, Doug Henson, and Luther Hooper. I couldn't believe our bad luck. Bobby and Doug were fine, but Mama had already warned me about Luther, and I hoped that Miss Daisy would catch on soon.

This year in Miss Daisy's room, we spent each morning in work groups. She structured the whole year as an imaginary trip around the world, and each morning the groups planned a coming part of the trip. Miss Daisy herself bounced around the room from group to group. She must have known that almost all of us already knew each other very well because she put one of the new boys in each of the three work groups. My group got Bobby Hannah, and I surely was glad that Luther Hooper did not end up with us. This meant that I hardly had any closeup contact with him for the whole year.

This year with Miss Daisy turned out to be my favorite of all school years so far. We did so much and learned so much on our imaginary travels that each day went by before we were ready for it, and the year itself seemed that it had hardly started when winter was coming to an end and spring was in the air.

Since Daddy and Mama had both grown up on farms and had also both lived through the Depression, they did not trust the permanence of the jobs they had. Daddy reminded us that, yes, he worked at the bank, but one of the two banks in town had closed during the Depression. And Mama told us that in some states

On the way to church about 1950, with Daddy and Joe

close to us not all of the schools had managed to open in some years of the Depression. So we needed to be prepared and able to take care of ourselves if worst came to worst. This meant that we had Helen, our Guernsey milk cow, and we had both a big garden for vegetables and a flock of chickens for meat and eggs.

As spring approached, it was time to order our baby chickens for the year. After they arrived, the baby chicks lived in the kitchen until they were old enough to take out and add to the flock of grown-up chickens. This was a touchy time, as the half-grown ones had no size or instinct to protect them if a fox or a weasel should get into the chicken lot before they were full grown. By that time, they would be fairly safe, but we worried about them when they first were put outside in the springtime.

That day came, and the half-grown pullets went out to live with all the rest of the hens in the lot at the chicken house against the end of Helen's barn. It was easy that way to feed them and gather the eggs when Daddy went to milk. I didn't mind feeding the chickens when he asked me, but I hated gathering the eggs.

Some old hens were always sitting on their nests when I went to gather the eggs. I was supposed to reach under them and pull out the warm eggs, but some of them were mean and guaranteed to peck me if I tried to lift their eggs in this way.

One evening a week or two after the little chickens went outside to live, Daddy had returned from milking and we were eating supper. It was dusky dark outside when all of a sudden we heard a great squawking and cackling coming from the henhouse.

"Go quickly, Joe," Mama directed. "Something's in the henhouse. I was afraid this might happen. I'll bet you a nickel it's a little red fox."

Daddy didn't need to be told; he was already on the way. He pulled his big shotgun out of the closet beside the stove in the kitchen and loaded it as he headed out the back door.

"Be careful, Joe!" Mama admonished as he disappeared into the dusk.

In less than a minute, we heard the shotgun go off. *Blam, blam*—there were two shots. Back in the kitchen where we were, Mama was wringing her hands. Guns for any reason always scared her to death.

It was only about five more minutes until Daddy came back into the house.

"What was it?" Mama could not wait for him to tell us on his own.

"One little weasel," he answered. "I am totally sure of that!"

"Did you kill it?" This was my question.

"No, I didn't kill it. But I sure scared the life out of it, and it is a sure thing that that little weasel will not come back around here again!"

"I am so relieved," Mama went on. "Did the weasel get any of our little chickens? You know, once they get the taste of blood, there is nothing you can do to keep them from wanting to get it again."

"I don't think it actually made it into the chicken house. When I scared it off, it was already running around the barn and out of sight. No, it's not going to be back around here."

That settled it. We went on to bed, and I remembered the event but did not really give more thought to it.

The next afternoon, Daddy got home from work and changed his clothes so he could go on out to the barn and milk before supper was ready. He milked twice a day, so I really paid no attention to the whole process. On this day, however, he came looking for me before he headed out to the barn. "Come go to milk with me, son. I want to show you something about that little weasel that was here last night."

Since I often went to milk with him, I fell in beside his steps, and we walked the fifty yards or so down in the pasture to the barn beside the creek.

The first business was milking Helen. I fumbled around, kicking clods and hay, while Daddy milked. He had tried several times to teach me to milk, and though I was gradually getting the hang of it, he was never patient enough with either me or Helen to turn the job over to me. He was a strong and fast milker.

Once he was finished, he spoke to me. "Come around here, son. I don't think this particular weasel was even looking for chickens to eat. Let me show you what he was after."

We walked around the barn to the side next to the chicken house. Daddy's old pushcart was turned upside down so it would not fill with rainwater while it was not being used. There was the pushcart in its normal storage place, but both wheels were missing!

"See," Daddy said, "this little weasel wasn't wanting to make a chicken dinner. He was wanting to make some kind of wagon or cart."

"It wasn't a weasel at all. Why did you tell Mama that it was a weasel? You say that we always have to tell the truth."

"It was an actual weasel, son. Go look up the word in the dictionary. I think that you will discover that one meaning of the word *weasel* will be something like, 'a scoundrel or a deceitful or treacherous person.' I believe that whoever did this is all of those things, so he is truly and truthfully a weasel."

I looked up at Daddy. "I know who did it!" I told him. "I know this little weasel's actual name."

The name was on my lips when Daddy stopped me. "Now, son," he started calmly, "you may think you know, but you did not see him, and I saw only a flash of his backside as he ran around the barn into the dark. You have to have some good, hard evidence if you're going to accuse somebody of something. Let's just say you think you might know, but we have to leave it at that. Don't go out on a limb without actual evidence, even if that's a hard thing to do."

I listened, but I still thought I knew who did it.

"Let's go on back to the house. Mama will wonder why we are staying out here so long."

We started through the pasture when suddenly Daddy stopped and bent down. He picked something up that had been dropped there in the tall pasture grass. It was an old, rusty monkey wrench, the kind with wooden sides on the handle, right there in our pasture.

"Look at this. Looks like the little weasel dropped his wrench! I bet I scared him good, all right." Daddy put the wrench in his overalls pocket. "Don't say anything about any of this when we get back to the house. Stuff like this upsets your mama, and we don't want to do that!" He gave me a big wink, and I knew that we had a safe secret between us.

It was a hard thing to go back to school the next day and look at Luther. I was sure that he was the one who had done it. But in keeping with Daddy's rules, neither one of us had seen him, and there was not what Daddy called "actual evidence" to go along with what I thought. I just had to live with it.

Every day in Miss Daisy's room, we pretended to make more progress with our trip around the world. We would come to a new country and even cook and eat some of the food she taught us came from that country. One of my favorites was when we got to Brazil and we cooked tapioca and learned about the cassava plant and how the people had to rinse all the poison out to get the good tapioca to eat in the end. We learned every day.

Every night at supper, Mama would ask me the same question: "What did you learn at school today?" I hated the question, but this year in Miss Daisy's class it was a lot easier to answer, and I usually went to sleep at night still thinking of things we had learned during that day.

Daddy had another question. It was harder to answer, but somehow it was not as annoying as Mama's repeated query. "What do you think you learned today that nobody else in your class learned?" I could think a long time about this, and usually Daddy and I talked about it as I was trying to figure out the answer. I did not figure out that he was teaching me more with this question than I had already learned during the day.

The year moved on. It was getting toward the end of Miss Daisy's imaginary trip when we traveled down the Nile River and came out through Egypt into the Mediterranean Sea. There was a lot to learn about the pharaohs and all the history of the Egyptians before we got out for the year.

One day, we were trying to figure out how the Egyptians got the foundations of the pyramids level when they were building them. With Miss Daisy's help, we figured it out. When we went outside for recess, she got a shovel and mattock from Haskell Davis, our janitor. She had us dig a square trench on the playground in the shape we thought would do for a pyramid. Then she got the water hose that Haskell used to wash off the sidewalk behind the lunchroom, and she had us fill the trench up with water.

All of a sudden, we realized that while one side of the square ditch was not yet full to the top, water was running over on the other side. We had to dig the ditch deeper until we got it deep enough that there was water all the way around the ditch.

"Now," she pointed out, "the top of the water is level all the way around. So you would have to dig the high part down until it is all even with the water level to get the foundation right."

It was totally obvious when she did it. Why didn't we think of that?

Miss Daisy told us all about a set of ancient discoveries called "the simple machines." Just about everything that has been invented has been based on some combination of the simple machines. The whole class loved this part.

We learned about the wheel, the lever, the inclined plane. It all made sense to us. Some of the kids who didn't like arithmetic loved this part because it made sense of a lot of tools they used at home on the farms.

At the end of the day, Miss Daisy gave us a challenge. "Here is your homework for tonight. When you get home, I want you to tell your parents about what we learned about the Egyptians and the simple machines. Then I want you to go all over your house trying to find examples of simple machines that we still use to make our lives easier today. Here's the real challenging part. I want to see if each one of you can bring something small from home tomorrow, something that is an example of a simple machine that you have not really noticed before. We will go through them, and you can each explain what you brought. Then we will put them over here on this table and keep them there until Friday, so we can have time to look at what everybody brought. That's your assignment."

When I got home that night, I was ready for Daddy to ask his favorite question: "What did you learn today that you think no one else learned?"

"Well," I started, "we learned all about simple machines. And we are supposed to look around our houses for examples of simple machines that make our lives easier. Tomorrow, we are supposed to bring something from home that illustrates a simple machine and explain it to the class."

"Yes," Daddy smiled, "but what did you learn that nobody else learned?"

I was ready. "Well, we talked about the simple machines one at a time. But when I think about it, I think that some of the most important things are when you put two simple machines together to make one thing that works in a way that neither one of them could work alone."

"What's an example?" Daddy would not quit.

"I thought of a nut and bolt. It is a combination of a wheel and axle plus an inclined plane. The nut turns around the bolt like a wheel, but since the grooves on the bolt angle up like an inclined plane, the nut gets tighter or looser depending on which way you turn it. Is that a good guess?"

"It's not a guess," Daddy said, smiling. "You are absolutely right."

"I think I will take a nut and bolt and tell how it is two things at once."

We went to look through the junk in the garage to see if we could find a large bolt and nut so that what I wanted to show would be easy to see. Daddy was as interested in this project as I was. He kept pulling out boxes and buckets and tin cans that had all kinds of stuff in them.

All of a sudden, we hit pay dirt. Right there in an old toolbox was the rusty monkey wrench we had found on the ground the night the wheels had been stolen from the pushcart. It was what Daddy had jokingly said had been dropped by the little weasel as he was scared away by the shotgun blast.

"Take this." Daddy picked up the old monkey wrench. "See, when you adjust the wrench to make it smaller or larger, you are turning a wheel around an axle, and it is going up or down a circular inclined plane. That's what makes it get larger or smaller."

I picked up the old wrench. This would be perfect!

The following day, I went to school with my chosen example of what can happen if you put together two simple machines. Miss Daisy was thrilled not only with my wrench but that many in the class had done what I had done: they had brought tools and devices that were the result of putting more than one of the simple machines together. William Birchfield had, for example, brought his mother's can opener. It had a lever on one end that was pointed and pierced the top of a drink can (William said his daddy called this part "the church key"), while the other end actually had two wheels and axles, one sharp wheel that cut around the rim of the can and a wheel that you turned by its handle to make the sharp wheel work.

We had a wonderful display of machines. Later in the day, we each told about what we had brought and then put them all on a small table, where they could be studied and examined by all for the rest of the week.

That night, Daddy asked again, "What do you think you learned that nobody else in your class learned?"

I had an answer: "I learned that there are other kids in my class who are just as smart as I am, especially those who have grown up working with tools on the farm."

Daddy liked this answer.

All week, we continued to examine the tools that were brought. There was a pencil sharpener (another wheel-and-axle device), a screwdriver, several doorstops, a window sash pulley—all kinds of things.

On Friday afternoon, Miss Daisy told us again what a good job we had done with the simple machines and about how the Greeks and Egyptians would be proud of us. Then she said, "We have had all of these examples here long enough, so when the bell rings today, as you leave to go home, I want each person to go to the table and take home what belongs to you. Don't forget to thank your parents for helping you with this."

Eventually, the end-of-school bell rang. I was never in a hurry to leave when the bell rang because, unlike those who were bus riders, I had to wait for my mama to finish all her work so I could ride home with her. By the time I got back to the table, almost everyone else had gathered belongings and was gone out the door.

I looked for the monkey wrench, knowing exactly where I had put it, but it was gone! This was not upsetting. After all, it was old and rusty and was not really ours to begin with,

I headed out in the hall toward Mama's room. At the end of the hall, the last pupils from my classroom were crowding out the door. That's when I saw the monkey wrench—it was being carried out the door in Luther Hooper's hand!

I did not say a word, just walked into Mama's room and waited for her to finish. Finally, we gathered everything up and headed to the car and then on home. Mama did not need in any way to know what I knew.

Daddy came home later, and soon we all sat down for supper. After the food was passed around, Mama asked her daily question: "What did you learn at school today?"

"Aw, Mama, today was Friday. You don't learn anything on Friday. All you do is go over the week and think about how there is not going to be any school for the next two days."

She did not look happy with my answer.

Then it was Daddy's turn: "Okay, son, what did you learn today that nobody else in your class learned?"

I looked straight at him and said it: "I learned for sure the little weasel's name!"

Cripple Joe

Even in the small town of Waynesville, there were several Joe Davises. This meant that nicknames were involved in being sure you were talking about the right one. There was a farmer out on the edge of town whom everyone called "Joe Silas," keeping his middle name intact, to be sure everyone knew about whom they were speaking. There was Joe Woodrow Davis, a photographer in Hazelwood, whom I often heard people call "Kodak Joe." And then there was my daddy.

Daddy and Mr. Jim Noland were the embodiment of the loan department at First National Bank. Daddy knew everybody in Haywood County who had ever needed a loan at the bank. And for this reason, his community nickname was "Banker Joe."

I loved this nickname, as it quite often brought a bit of attention to me. I would meet someone, especially an adult, who would ask me, "Who's your daddy, son?"

I would answer, "Joe Davis."

"Which one?"

"Banker Joe."

The questioner would usually then tell me about how my daddy had loaned them money for one thing or another and what a fine man he was for doing this. It seemed like they thought I was going to go right home and tell my daddy about their compliments so they would be held in better stead the next time they wanted to borrow some money at the bank.

I was thirteen years old. It was a day when Mama was going to the Ladye Faire Beauty Parlor and did not want me tagging along complaining about not wanting to be there. So, as happened so many times, I was dropped off at the bank to stay the day out with Daddy until it was time for him to go home.

This turned out to be another one of those days when it was Daddy's turn to close up the bank after all the other employees left for home. I went around with him as we made sure all the lights were off, the windows closed, and the back door locked. Then I watched while he wound the time clocks in the back side of the vault door. He let me close the big vault door, spin the wheel that looked like it could steer a riverboat, and whirl the two combination dials until the vault was secure. I loved to do this. Now, we were ready to go out the front door and head for home.

He and I stepped out onto the sidewalk, and he turned and put the key in the door lock. The lock clicked shut, and we started to walk away. At that moment, Mr. Pitt McCarroll came out of his furniture store, which was directly across the street. Of course, he and Daddy knew one another. I knew him, too, as I went to school with his sons, Steve and Rick.

Daddy spoke first. "Good night, Pitt. Hope you have a good supper and a good night of sleep."

Mr. McCarroll replied, "I hope you do, too, Cripple Joe!"

And that was that. We headed on to Daddy's Plymouth, parked around at the side of the bank next to Bill Balentine's Shell station.

We both got into the car. I sat there while Daddy put the key in the ignition and started the Plymouth. Then I couldn't hold it any longer. My thirteen-year-old's anger burst out. "I didn't like that!"

"You didn't like what?"

"I didn't like what Mr. McCarroll called you."

"What did he call me? I guess I wasn't paying attention." Daddy looked innocent.

"He called you 'Cripple Joe.' He is supposed to call you 'Banker Joe.' "

Daddy laughed. "So he did, did he? And you've never heard that before? Let me tell you a little story."

The Plymouth had started backing out of its parking place while this conversation was going on. Now, I was aware that Daddy shifted the car out of reverse and into low gear as we pulled back into the parking space where we had started. He pulled on the emergency brake and turned off the engine. I guessed this meant that we were going to be here for a while.

The beginnings of his story I already knew. He reviewed what the whole family knew was our history. Daddy had been born in 1901, the eighth child in a family on a farm still being chopped out of the wilderness in the Iron Duff township in the north end of Haywood County. Then he got specific.

He told me that it was 1906, and he was five years old. His father (my grandfather) and his older brothers Moody and Harry were splitting cedar shingles to put a new roof on a little corncrib that was on the back side of the big barn.

Daddy said that he was fascinated by the tools. "They were using a froe and several wedges to split the lengths of cedar to start with. And there was a big, two-handled draw knife for cleaning up the shingles."

The most interesting thing to him was a small, short-handled ax that was being used for all kinds of trimming work a larger tool was not needed for. "That little ax was fascinating to me," he went on. "It was almost like a large hatchet and looked like it was just the right size for me. I wanted to get my hands on it and try it out. It was stuck into the end of the split log that was used to hold the cedar in place while they worked to split it. When I tried to pull

The children, from left to right with their parents, are Uncle Harry, Uncle Moody, Aunt Esther, Daddy, Aunt Mary, and Uncle Frank. The photo was taken about 1909, when Daddy was about eight years old.

it out of the log and play with it, Daddy told me to keep my little hands off of it. He said that it was sharp enough to shave with and was very dangerous—more dangerous, he said, than a full-sized ax. He told me to leave it alone."

He kept watching the work and eyeing the little ax. After a good while, my grandmother (his mama) called all of them to come to the house for dinner. Dinner was always the noon meal on the farm, as the workers needed the biggest meal then to power them for the afternoon's work.

Granddaddy and Uncle Moody and Uncle Harry put down their tools and started for the house. Daddy lingered. All of a sudden, he knew that this would be his chance to get his hands on the forbidden ax, even if just for a few minutes. So he dawdled and fell behind as they headed to the house.

As soon as all three of them were safely out of sight, he walked over to the big log. He grabbed the little ax by its handle and easily pulled it out of the log. Then he told me that he started chopping everything in sight. He chopped pieces of wood. He chopped little sprouts that were growing out of the ground. He even tried to see if he could split one of the big pieces of cedar. He was five years old.

About that time, his mama realized that little Joe had not come to dinner. All the others were washed and ready to sit down and eat, but he was not there. She stuck her head out the door of the house and hollered for him again: "Come to dinner, Joe. We're all waiting for you!"

At that moment, he knew that he better get going. If one of his parents had to come looking for him, he would be in trouble, especially if they found him playing with the ax he had been told not to touch. So he got ready to chop the ax back into the log and run for the house.

Now in a hurry, Daddy ran over to the big log and gave the ax a quick swing to chop it into the wood where it stayed when not being used. He didn't aim carefully, and when he swung the ax it glanced off the corner of the log, and the blade buried itself in an instant deep through the kneecap of his left knee and into the joint. This is the way the rest of the family found him on the ground when they finally went out to see why little Joe had not come to dinner.

My grandfather called to my grandmother to bring some clean sheets. He then yanked the ax out of Daddy's leg and carried him to the house, where my grandmother tightly bound his leg with the sheets while my grandfather ran back to the barn to saddle one of the horses.

Granddaddy got Daddy up on the horse and rode him to the nearest country doctor's house. When that doctor unwrapped Daddy's leg and saw what had happened, he just stood there and stared at it. Then he said, "I have never seen anything like this before. I don't know what to do, way out here without being at a hospital. The only thing I know to do is to take his leg off."

Granddaddy got Daddy back onto the horse, and they rode

into Waynesville and went to the train depot. "When is the next train coming, and where is it going?" Granddaddy asked the station agent.

The good news was that the next train was coming in just over an hour. The bad news was that the train was not going east toward Asheville, only about thirty miles away. It was going west to the end of the Southern Railway line in Murphy. Murphy was smaller than Waynesville, and there were no hospitals west of Asheville.

"But," the agent told Granddaddy, "from the Southern Railway station on the east side of Murphy, you could take a carriage through town to the L&N station on the west side of town, and from there you could get a train to Atlanta. They try to make those trains so that the schedules fit together, so it might work."

Granddaddy bought two tickets to Atlanta and laid Daddy down on one of the wooden benches in the train station.

My grandfather was in the North Carolina legislature for multiple terms between 1890 and his death in 1920. In fact, in 1909, he introduced a bill that brought prohibition to North Carolina a decade before the Volstead Act made it the law of the nation. But on that particular day, he left the train station and knew exactly where to go to buy a quart of homemade moonshine whiskey. In only a few minutes, he was back in the station with the whiskey in hand.

Daddy told me that his father then began to give him little doses of "medicine." At first, the whiskey choked him, and he coughed and gagged and wheezed. "Then," he went on, "I got kind of used to it, and it took my mind off of how bad my leg hurt. In a little while, I had had so much medicine that I went to sleep, or somewhere!" He told me that he had no memory at all of the 172-mile train ride to Atlanta. He was out for the entire trip.

Finally, Granddaddy somehow got Daddy to Atlanta and located the new Grady Hospital. That is where they saved Daddy's leg. "They took off my kneecap," he told me, "then they kept my whole knee laid open and kept irrigating it so that it wouldn't develop blood poisoning." His leg eventually healed, leaving him without a kneecap but with a deep scar into which a large man's thumb could disappear. That leg ended up slightly shorter as he grew, and his knee had only the slightest ability to bend for the rest of his life.

Daddy did not remember how long he had stayed in the hospital. He told me that he didn't know what kind of medicine they gave him for the pain and that he was passed out a lot of the time. But finally, the ordeal was over, and they took the trip back home.

"Once back home," he went on, "I became one of the girls. I couldn't do anything that my brothers were capable of doing on the farm. And it was obvious that I would grow up unable to handle the horses with plowing or mowing. I couldn't handle heavy equipment."

My grandmother taught him to knit, and he became the family sock knitter. At first, she taught him to knit straight socks that just had the end sewed up. It sounded like what I would have called tube socks. When he got good at that, she taught him how to slow down and put in the heels. He told me he was a very good sock knitter.

He learned to spin flax as well as wool and was very proud that, as far as flax spinning was concerned, he was better than two of his three sisters. (When he was in his seventies, we took him to Colonial Williamsburg. While there, we happened to stop in on a flax demonstration at the George Wythe House. Right in the middle of things, he interrupted the interpreter and told her that she had two of the steps in the wrong order! She kindly invited him to tell the audience all about it, and he stood up and took them through flax production from growing to retting to scutching to hackling, right on to spinning, dyeing, and weaving. He had grown up with it.)

By now, I was totally captivated by the story. Daddy told me that by the time he was my age he had realized that he was going to have to find a way to make money that "didn't involve work." He could not manage the heavy farm chores.

Since Granddaddy was in the legislature, he subscribed to several newspapers to keep up with things. In one of these newspapers, Daddy read that down in Charlotte, North Carolina, there was a little school called King's Business College, where they would teach you to make a living without working. (His only definition of *work* was manual farm labor.)

All through his high-school years, he did little odd jobs and saved his money. He made socks and sold them. He did spinning for women who wanted to get on to the weaving and dyeing part. He even did a lot of work measuring fields for farmers and then calculating for them how much seed or fertilizer they would need for certain crops in certain fields.

In 1918, Daddy was graduated from Haywood Institute in Clyde. He was seventeen years old. At the end of that summer, he took all of his savings and went to town. There, he bought a train ticket to Charlotte, found King's Business College in the upstairs of a building on West Trade Street, and told them he wanted to go to school there.

The person to whom he talked counted Daddy's money and sadly informed him that he did not have enough money to pay for one term of school. Daddy begged them to let him come on to school and stay just until his money ran out. He would work hard and learn as much as he could. The school agreed, and he began to learn about business.

Uncle Moody, one of Daddy's older brothers, had just returned from World War I. He had been a fireman in the army in France. Daddy found the Charlotte fire station on South Boulevard and met the firemen. He told them all about his brother who was a fireman in the war and told them about how he had come to Charlotte to go to school because of what he had done to his leg. The firemen took him in and invited him to sleep in the upstairs of the fire station. He never had to rent a room or pay rent while he was there in school.

Before the end of the first term at King's Business College, they came to him and told him that it was time for him to go home.

All the money was not gone, but they advised him to go home anyway. "They told me"—he was speaking very softly now—"that in less than that first term I had learned as much about typing, shorthand, bookkeeping, and business as they usually taught in two years." He insisted, "I had to learn it. The money was running out!"

So, without ever having a piece of paper to show that he had been to school, he returned home to Haywood County. In Waynesville, down by the train depot, two old men, Mr. Blackwell and Mr. Bushnell, had a wholesale grocery company. Through the years, they had run the business singlehandedly, the two of them doing all of the physical and office work. Daddy went to them and convinced them that if they hired him to be their bookkeeper, he thought he could save them more money than it would cost them to pay him. They tried him out, and indeed it worked. He was, as he said, "making a living without working."

The following year, 1920, his father died. It was before life insurance and before Social Security. Daddy's inheritance was simple. The older siblings, Moody and Harry and Grover and Flora, were all grown up and gone out into the world with lives of their own. At age nineteen, Daddy was the oldest one who was not married. So he inherited five little brothers and sisters who now had no father, as well as the care of his widowed mother and unmarried aunt Laura, who was a permanent member of the household.

For the next twenty years, he worked and raised the children, worked and took care of his mother, worked and looked out for Aunt Laura. It was the same cycle over and over again. In the end, four of the five siblings went to college and were safely launched into the world.

Daddy's story seemed to be slowing now with deliberateness. "I got to be forty years old, and I had forgotten to get married."

Daddy told me that in 1941, Mr. Jim Boyd, who had founded First National Bank in Waynesville and kept it open through the Depression when other banks had closed, decided that it was time for him to let go of the bank. It was bought out, and Mr. Jonathan Woody, who had grown up in Cataloochee Valley, became the new president of the bank. "Mr. Woody came to me and told me he wanted me to come to work at the bank," Daddy went on. "He wanted me to be in charge of the loan department. When I asked him why he wanted me, he said, 'Because you are cripple. You see, Joe, anybody who needs to borrow money is at that time in their life cripple in some way. Since you are cripple, you will be the one who can understand them.'"

So he went to work at the bank. And when Daddy met my mama, when he was forty-two and she was twenty-three, he was already "Banker Joe."

By now, it was dark in the Plymouth. I could see Daddy sitting there talking with me like a silhouette in the dark. He was looking straight at me. "Don't you see, son? Don't you see? If I had not gotten to be Cripple Joe, I would never have gotten to be Banker Joe. If I had not gotten to be Cripple Joe, I would be plowing with mules down in Iron Duff, and you would probably be in trouble with every teacher you've got. You have to be very careful not to be broken or even discouraged when something the world thinks is bad happens to you. You see, just like with me, if you can learn to use trouble right, it just might buy you a ticket to a place you would never, ever have gotten to go any other way."

After that day, it was fine with me if people still called Daddy "Banker Joe," but what I really liked was to meet someone who knew his whole story well enough to call out, "Hello, Cripple Joe!"

This is the story I heard once from my father when I was thirteen years old. I took in the story, and it did have a lesson for me, but there were things about it that I had not the maturity to ask at that age. Much later on, I began to reflect on the story with a great deal of wonder.

How did he actually come to understand what had happened to him? Why did the accident not simply ruin him for the rest of his life? Why was he not possessed with the demon of a split-second foolish injury that changed the entire prospect for his future? Simply put, how did he come to understand that Cripple

Joe had given him the gift of a life he could not have had if he had walked away from the ax and followed his brothers to dinner?

When my father was ninety-two years old, I heard the rest of the story.

I did not know that I was visiting him on the last Christmas of his life. The following October, he would depart from this earth. We were talking in the living room in front of the fireplace when suddenly I remembered the time he had talked into the darkness to tell me the story of Cripple Joe. Now, I was ready to ask him about it.

"Dad," I started, "I was just thinking about that time that Mr. McCarroll called you 'Cripple Joe' and I didn't like it. That's when you told me the story of what happened to your leg. Do you remember telling me that?"

"Of course. We were sitting in the car behind the bank. I wanted to sit there alone with you so I was sure that you listened to it. You must have listened to it if you still remember it."

"I remember it a lot of times. But now I have a question about it: how did you come to understand what happened to you that way? I don't understand how you learned that being cripple was not a tragedy—in fact, that it wasn't even something that was going to hurt you."

There was a smile on his face, like he had been waiting thirty-five years for me to ask this question.

He started, "It was my mother, your grandmother, who did it. You never knew her at all. She died in November before you were born in June. She's the one who did it."

I was listening.

"It wasn't long after I got back home from the hospital when one day she called me to come and sit down at the kitchen table while she was fixing supper. She looked at me and said, 'Joe, now that your leg's healed up, it's time for you to tell the story.'

" 'What story?' I asked her.

" 'The story of what happened to you and your leg.'

"I objected," he said. "I told her that I didn't want to tell that story because telling the story couldn't change what happened.

"She looked right at me and said, 'Joe, you're not telling the story to change what happened, you're telling the story to change you!' She told me that if I didn't tell the story that what happened would sit on top of me like a rock until it squashed all of the hope and all of the joy and all of the life out of me. She told me that if I didn't learn to tell the story, I would be a pitiful old cripple man by the time I was forty years old, and that nobody would want to be around me or live with me. I remember she said, 'Telling the story doesn't change the things that happened, but telling it can change the person it happened to.' So I told the story.

"About a month later, she called me down again. 'Joe, it's time for you to tell the story again. This time, I want you to tell it and tell what you think you learned by living through all of that.'

"Over the next years, I can't tell you how many times she had me tell that story. But every time, her directions were different. 'Joe, tell what happened to your leg, and tell what your father and I learned by going through that with you. . . . Joe, tell about your leg, and tell what you think the nurses and doctors at the hospital thought about while they were taking care of you. . . . Joe, tell the story, and tell it the way you would want a child of yours to hear it if you ever have children.' "

He didn't stop talking but went on, "One day, when I was about as old as you were when I told you the part in the car, she called me to the kitchen table and said, 'Joe, I want you to tell the story, and tell what you get to do because of your leg that your brothers Moody, Harry, and Frank don't get to do.'

"I thought about it for a moment and realized that I got to stay in the house and read and study and help Mama while they were out plowing with the horses. I got to figure out all about how much seed we needed of every kind and how much of different crops we needed to grow to feed the family or to sell. That was the day I realized that chopping my leg might have been the best thing I had ever done in my life." His smile was huge.

"So," I said stupidly, "your mother was kind of like a therapist?"

"No!" he almost shouted. "If you go to a therapist, by definition you have something wrong and the therapist does not. You are not equals, but one of you is sick and the other one is well. My mother never, ever suggested or allowed me to suggest that I had anything wrong with me. Nor did she ever suggest that she knew the answer to anything. She put it all on me. It was my job to tell my way out from under the rock and sit up on top of the story."

So now I knew the whole story. And I knew that in spite of college and university degrees I had managed to accumulate along the way, I had just learned a whole new degree's worth through my father from that grandmother I never met.

Farther Along

My father loved being in charge of things. For that reason, there were two areas of life he enjoyed perhaps more than anything else.

He loved his job at the bank. His position in the installment loan department fit his personality perfectly. He got to assess his clients' financial and life situations and make decisions that affected them in deep and important ways. He took this job very seriously and believed that if a customer of his got into financial difficulty, he was surely partly to blame. People respected and loved the way he handled his job.

The other place where he really got to exercise his enjoyment of being in charge was as the Sunday-school song leader. Daddy loved to sing, and every Sunday he was the one who got to pick out the hymns that we all sang at the general assembly of the Methodist Sunday-school hour at church.

He did not sing in the choir, nor would he. That was because if you sang in the choir you had to sing the songs that Mrs. Florence

Martin, the choir director, picked out. No, he liked being the one who made the choices.

When we got to church on Sunday mornings, the first thing that happened was the Sunday-school general assembly at nine forty-five. All ages, children and their parents, gathered in the sanctuary of the church for this opening time. Mrs. Bowles played the piano in the sanctuary as people arrived, then Daddy announced and led the opening hymn. After the opening hymn, there were announcements and birthdays. We then sang a second hymn while the Sunday-school offering was taken up. Then there was the benediction, and we went at ten o'clock to all of our age-level classes until ten forty-five.

At home on Sunday mornings, I would always hear him trying out hymns for the day as he shaved and got dressed for church. I can still hear his strong lead voice as he would start several songs just to feel how they sounded for the day. He told us he had to see what fit the weather and the mood of the day.

"I have found a friend in Jesus, he's everything to me.... Blessed assurance, Jesus is mine. . . . Standing on the promises of Christ, my king . . . I will sing of my Redeemer. . . ." I can close my eyes and easily hear him singing in the bathroom on Sunday morning.

There was one song that he seemed to love more than all the rest, and it seems to me like we sang it about once every other month. Maybe it was that this song captured the questions and faith of his own heart, but he did dearly love it:

> *Tempted and tried, we're oft made to wonder*
> *Why it should be thus all the day long;*
> *While there are others living about us,*
> *Never molested, though in the wrong.*

Then came the chorus:

> *Farther along we'll know more about it,*
> *Farther along we'll understand why;*

Cheer up, my brother, live in the sunshine,
We'll understand it all by and by.

He did love that song.

I was eight years old and in the third grade at Hazelwood School. It was 1953. One evening, we were just sitting down for our supper when Daddy said to Mama, "You will never believe what happened at work today."

"If I won't believe it, then you better just tell me," she smiled.

"Clarence Shelton came in the bank and wanted to borrow money to buy a new Buick."

I sat up and listened. Everyone in town knew who Clarence Shelton was, even an eight-year-old. Clarence was the one and only orderly at the Haywood County Hospital, and Clarence Shelton was a black man.

Part of the reason that I knew this was that Clarence did not look black to a child. He had very fair skin, freckles, and almost reddish hair. I am sure that I had probably asked questions about Clarence and had it made clear to me that he was "not like us." Either one of my parents would have politely told me to call him "a colored man."

Daddy's story went on. "Yes, Clarence came in the bank to talk to me. He showed me that he had right there in his hand enough cash money to pay Euell Taylor outright for the new Buick that he wanted to buy. But instead of paying the whole thing, he wanted me to loan him one-fourth of the total so he could build up a credit record. He wanted to go ahead and give me as much money as he wanted to borrow, so I would know for sure that he had the intention and ability to pay it back. I've never seen or heard of anything like it in all my life."

I was listening carefully now.

Mama looked almost shocked. "What did you do, Joe?"

"I loaned him the money. It was a good loan."

At the time, I did not know what a big thing I was hearing about. As I listened, I heard Daddy go on and tell Mama what she probably knew all the time. The bank had never before made a loan to a person of African-American descent. This loan broke records of the past and potentially opened doors that had never been cracked before.

After that day, we could be riding around town and would sometimes see Clarence driving his wife in the new Buick. It was a red and white 1953 Buick Super and was quite beautiful. Daddy said that Clarence told him that he was not going to drive it to work at the hospital. No, he lived where he could walk to work over there. But he did want to drive his wife to church in style, and he wanted to be able to go see his mama and make her proud of him.

As a child, what I saw was that the Buick was always spotless. When I mentioned this to Daddy, he said, "I know he washes and waxes on it all the time. He even told me that he changes the oil in it the first Saturday of every month, whether it has been driven much or not. Can you believe that?"

About a month after Clarence got the new Buick, a man named Birdie Wheeler came into the bank. Birdie Wheeler was also a black man. He wanted to borrow money to open a little takeout sandwich shop down in Nineveh on Pigeon Street. Daddy listened to Birdie outline his plan while he tried to figure out what to do.

While he was listening, he told us that night, he got the idea. He said to Birdie, "Well, that sounds pretty reasonable. But you know, we have to run all the figures and see how they turn out. Wait right here just a minute and let me check out the numbers."

Daddy told us that he left Birdie sitting there in the loan department while he got up and walked out of sight to the other side of the bank. Over there, he got on the telephone and called the hospital. He asked if he could speak to Clarence.

"Clarence, this is Joe at the bank. I need a little help. Birdie Wheeler is over here, and he wants to borrow some money to open a little takeout place in Nineveh. What do you think about it?"

In 1953, First National Bank in Waynesville celebrated its fiftieth anniversary. Dressed for the occasion, from left, are Jonathan Woody, president; J. H. Way, vice president and mayor of Waynesville; Jim Noland; and Daddy, the loan department and everything else!

Clarence cleared his throat. "Well, Mr. Joe, we've been needing a local place where you could pick up something to eat on the way home from work, and Birdie is just the man to do it. He was a cook in the army. Besides, he is a good and reliable man, and you can count on him to pay anything you loan him on time. I would swear on that."

Daddy hung up the phone and returned to the loan department.

"Well, Birdie, good news. All the numbers lined up right. All we've got to do now is have you sign a few papers, and I can get the check cut for you today. I'll come down there and try the place out as soon as you get up and going, so be sure to let me know. I believe I've heard that you were a cook in the army, weren't you?"

It wasn't long until a new business opened on Pigeon Street.

Only a few days later, another man—Daddy did not tell us his name—came into the bank. He was also a black man who wanted to borrow money for a project he had in mind. Daddy told us he listened to the man just like he listened to Birdie, then excused himself "to check and see if the numbers lined up."

This time, Clarence had a different response when Daddy told him the name of the man in question. "Don't give him a penny!" Clarence told Daddy. "He is a no-good scoundrel, and you might see the first payment, but then he is liable to disappear and leave you holding the bag. Don't give him anything!"

Glad for this important information, Daddy returned to the loan department. "I am very sorry," he reported to this applicant. "We ran all the numbers, and this just doesn't all line up. I am actually protecting you by not loaning you the money. I don't want you to get in a situation that you can't handle or that would be uncomfortable for you." He told us that this man, as he left the bank, actually thanked him for being so honest.

And so, unknown to anyone but us, Clarence Shelton, orderly at the hospital, had become the one-man clearing house for a whole new dimension of installment loan business that was being done through my daddy at the bank.

I noticed quite early that Daddy and Clarence began to refer to one another as Clarence and Joe. I also began to see that my father, who was born into a world clearly defined as black and white, was slowly beginning to learn to live in a world filled with color.

Every two years, Clarence would come back in the bank and make a new loan for his next new red Buick. He would borrow only one-fourth of what the trade was going to cost him, and he would hand to Daddy, in cash, the money it would take to pay off the loan. Daddy would then make the monthly payments from the cash Clarence had already given to him. Euell Taylor, the Buick dealer, told Daddy that he always had a list of people waiting to buy one of the Buicks that Clarence traded in, because they had almost no mileage on them and had been so perfectly cared for over his two years of ownership.

I also learned later on that no one whom Clarence cleared for a loan at the bank ever defaulted or was even late for a payment.

He had a perfect sense of the total pulse of his community.

Other than church, my father's chief outside activity was the Lions Club. He had been a member of Lions Clubs International for all of his adult life. When he died, the thing he wanted on his grave marker most was a medallion showing that he had been a Melvin Jones Fellow in Lions Clubs International. In all, he had nearly seventy years of perfect attendance with the Lions Club and was proud always of his fiftieth-anniversary perfect-attendance pin, which had a small diamond in it.

Daddy worked tirelessly for the Lions Club projects for the blind. Each year, I would go with him as he went from house to house all over his assigned part of Waynesville selling Industries for the Blind brooms and light bulbs to support the Lions' work with the blind. Hanging on the wall in our house throughout my whole childhood life was the plaque noting that he was president of the local Lions Club in 1946, when I was only two years old.

But it was the 1950s. In those days, there were two big ways in which the Lions Club raised money for the blind each year. One was the late-summer horse show. The other was the wintertime minstrel show. Daddy, working at the bank, was automatically the treasurer of both events.

The minstrel show was a blackface vaudeville-style show in which the white members of the Lions Club put on wigs, blacked their faces except for white makeup around their eyes and mouths, and pretended to be people they were never born to be. They would sing and dance and tell jokes and act patently stupid in blackface, doing things they would not have been caught dead doing in their normal daily activities. Daddy's role was often that of the black preacher, delivering his sermon in insulting dialect to howls of laughter.

Looking back, one of the strangest things about the minstrel shows was that everyone in town, black and white alike, bought tickets and filled the audience. It was Daddy's opinion that the black members of the audience made the show a whole lot better because they appreciated the humor more. It seemed to me later that the white Lions simply didn't know how much their antics were being laughed at by black attendees, who could not acceptably laugh at them in normal life. The minstrel shows were a hit all throughout my childhood years.

One year, Clarence came into the bank in early autumn to make his loan for a new Buick. The new models came out in September, and Euell Taylor made sure that there was a fully equipped red sedan at the opening of every odd-numbered year. This year, it would be a red and white Roadmaster.

Daddy and Clarence visited for a while, and then the loan was made with papers signed and cash swapped for a check. They then shook hands, and Clarence stood up to go. Daddy told us he had turned around and walked over to file the transaction when he heard Dr. N. F. Lancaster's voice. Dr. Lancaster was our family doctor, and he was a slight-framed, little man with a voice to match. His speech was stiltedly clear and unmistakable.

When Daddy turned around to speak to Dr. Lancaster, the doctor was nowhere in sight, but Clarence was still standing there.

"I thought I just heard Dr. Lancaster, Clarence. Was he here just a minute ago?"

Clarence smiled as he did not move. Then Daddy heard Dr. Lancaster's voice, but it was coming out of Clarence's mouth. "Oh, Clarence," he started, "that sure is another pretty Buick you got there." He was still smiling.

Daddy could not believe it. Clarence was an absolutely perfect mimic. Apparently, the people from Clarence's community who worked at the hospital knew he could do this, but my father was the first white person to be taken inside Clarence's secret talent.

"It was you, Clarence? It sounded just like Lancaster. How do you do that?"

"You can do *whatevah* you put your mind to, children!" This time, Clarence imitated Buck Bowles, the school superintendent. Daddy said he laughed all over himself.

Then Clarence looked at Daddy seriously. "Joe, that was just an audition."

"What do you mean, audition?"

"I was trying out for the minstrel show."

Then Clarence went on to explain to Daddy what he had in mind. He wanted the Lions to secretly black his face and put a wig on him and slip him anonymously into the minstrel show. They could advertise that they had a special guest star from out of town if they wanted to. He would then sing and dance with all the rest until the featured time came. He would then put on a little skit he called "Life in the Hospital," in which he would play the voice parts of the doctors, nurses, and patients, most of whom would be sitting right there in the audience.

To this day, I still have black-and-white photographs to prove that they did it! With his fair skin and freckles, Clarence was totally disguised by the blackface makeup. The addition of a wig to his mostly bald head completed the effect. No one, even close up, could tell who he was.

The night of the show arrived. There was a pit orchestra made up of about a dozen members of the high-school band, also in blackface. They played an overture, and the green stage curtains opened. With straw hats and canes, out danced the Lions, singing, "California, Here I Come." Clarence was right in the middle of the front row.

There were some jokes, a very poorly done ventriloquist act, and another song. And then the big announcement was made. Daddy was actually the master of ceremonies for the show, and he really played it up. "Here we have, from out of town, a special celebrity guest star. Presenting: 'Life in the Hospital.' "

We saw Clarence step forward, unknown to anyone else there. But it was Dr. Lancaster's voice that we all heard. Then it was Coach Weatherby's voice. Coach was the high-school principal and also the football coach. (He was also my Sunday-school teacher.) Clarence had them consulting for a few moments, planning an unidentified operation.

Then the scene moved to the operating room. It became clear that Coach had gone to the hospital for hemorrhoid surgery. Dr. Lancaster took a look at the needed surgery and said in a loud voice, "You're going to have to go to Asheville to get this done, Coach. I am not certified to do brain surgery!" The whole place rolled in laughter.

There were a few more moments involving Dr. Lancaster and Miss Winnie Kirkpatrick, the nurse everyone knew as "the Shot Lady." Then, in the midst of laughter that would not stop, the skit was over.

"More! More!" the entire audience shouted.

It was while they were still laughing and shouting that Clarence pulled off the curly wig and wiped enough of the makeup off his face that everyone could see who he was. There was a brief moment of surprised silence, then the applause and laughter started again, louder than ever. I thought it would never settle down.

It was the last-ever minstrel show. Everyone seemed silently to know that after that year there was no point in even trying it again. Once the unsurpassable climax had been reached by "Life in the Hospital," there was no point in even making an effort again. An era had quietly passed.

Daddy and Clarence continued to do business together until they had both retired, Daddy from the bank and Clarence from the hospital. Daddy was a few years older than Clarence. They remained friends forever after that. Daddy said once, "There's nothing like carrying secrets together that cements a friendship."

"Yeah," I said, "but in the end everyone knew it was Clarence in the minstrel show."

"You are right about that one," he went on. "But to this day, nobody knows who really approved or turned down a whole lot of installment loans." They were tight.

When my father passed his ninetieth birthday, he began to have small strokes. Since Mama was so much younger, she simply kept him at home and worked to care for him as well as possible. To most people who came for a visit, he seemed remarkably well for his age. But as soon as the company left, he returned to being unpredictable and difficult to manage. Gradually, his care was wearing her out, but she would not give up. The most difficult thing for her was somehow getting him bathed. Between her lack of physical strength and his lack of cooperation, it was almost impossible. The other difficulty was that she was afraid to leave him alone. Just out of her sight, he could end up far from where she knew him to be. Things were getting harder and harder.

One day, the telephone rang. When Mama answered, it was Clarence. "Just a minute, Clarence. I'll get Joe."

"No, Mrs. Davis, I don't want to talk to Joe. I was calling you. I keep hearing around town about how Joe is having some hard times, and I know that all of it is on you. Here's what I would like to do, if you will permit me. I'd like to make a plan with you to come and visit Joe when you need me to. Call me when you need to go to the grocery store or just when you want to go to the beauty shop. I know that my wife would rather go to the beauty shop than about anything. You don't even have to have a reason. Maybe you just want a little rest. So call me, and I will come out there and visit with Joe while you go and do whatever you want to do. You know that I have bathed him before when he was in the hospital. I am not too old to do that again. You would be surprised at the tricks I know to get people bathed who don't want to do it. You'll see what I can do."

About a week later, Mama took Clarence up on his offer. She was all ready with both a grocery list and a Ladye Faire Beauty Parlor appointment when the newest red Buick drove up our driveway hill. Mama said she met Clarence outside to thank him and ushered him into the house, where Daddy was watching television in the living room. On the way in, Clarence told her, "You don't even need to tell him you are leaving. Just leave him to me and take your time."

When Mama called to tell me the whole story, I could hear the smiles in her voice. "I think it was the first time in a year that I had left the house without a worry in this world. I knew he would be both safe and happy as long as Clarence was there." She said she went to the beauty shop, to Josephine's Dress Shop, to the Belk store, and finally to the grocery store before heading home.

The real story she had to tell me was about her arrival back home. She drove up the driveway and parked beside Clarence's Buick, then carried the first bag of groceries into the garage. She decided to bring all the bags of groceries there and then go inside to see how things were going before she put them all away in the kitchen.

When she opened the kitchen door, Mama could hear two distinct sounds coming from the other end of the house: one was the sound of water splashing, the other the sound of two old men singing.

As she walked cautiously through the living room and into the bedroom hallway, she was a little bit scared about what kind of mess she was going to find. Would there be water running out the bathroom door into the hall? It almost sounded like it.

She turned the corner, and there was the scene. Daddy was in the bathtub. Clarence was kneeling down on the floor beside it. He had a scrub brush, and he was washing Daddy's back as water splashed everywhere and he harmonized tenor to Daddy's strong lead voice:

> *Farther along we'll know more about it,*
> *Farther along we'll understand why;*
> *Cheer up, my brother, live in the sunshine,*
> *We'll understand it all by and by.*

As Mama finished telling me the story, all I could think was that, through an unlikely friendship of more that forty years, both Daddy and Clarence had surely come much "farther along."

Goldie Goldie

The first place I remember living was the house on Plott Creek Road. As I grew up, my assumption was that Mama and Daddy had lived there forever, just like my grandparents had lived in their old house forever. Later on, I discovered that my parents had moved into the Plott Creek house less than six months before I was born.

It was an old house when we lived there. Daddy said he heard that it was built around 1900. It was a true bungalow frame structure with the roofline coming down in front over the porch. In the back, there had once been a similar porch, but some owner before us had closed in about a third of this back porch and made the one bathroom we lived with in this house.

The house was on about a half-dozen acres of land that included our cow pasture, barn, and chicken house. There was also the garden on the other side of the house and its double row of apple trees. In the back of the house were the wooden garage and an old smokehouse that we used for storage, even though it made anything put therein smell like greasy and salty pork. There was a well in the backyard that was no longer a source of water for the house but scared Mama to death. She was certain that one of us was going to fall down the well and never be seen again. Her solution to this fear was to use the well as a trash depository. As the years passed, it was gradually filled to the top and would today likely be seen as an archaeological site to be uncovered.

From my earliest memory, I knew that we were not going to live in that house forever. "We're going to move!" was an assertion I heard again and again to accompany any discomfort, from heat in the summer to cold in the winter to not enough room for whatever. The only questions were where and when.

By the time I reached the sixth grade, the impetus to move was growing stronger and stronger. Mama would cut house plans out of magazines and look at them with Daddy. She would sometimes show a plan to Uncle Mark and ask him to "just guess" at what it would take to build it, since he was in the building supply business. Her request was always, "What do you think it would take to do it in brick veneer?" I never knew what that meant.

We also spent some time now and then visiting houses that Daddy knew to be for sale, whether they were officially advertised or not. Working in installment loans at the bank gave him a lot of inside information on what was going on in the housing market in Waynesville.

That year when I was twelve years old, I had no idea that one of the things Daddy was doing at work was partly supervising the house-building project of our family doctor, Dr. N. F. Lancaster. Dr. Lancaster was nearing retirement age and wanted to build the house he and Mrs. Lancaster would enjoy for the rest of their lives. He had chosen the plan and hired Don Crawford, a most respected Haywood County homebuilder, to build the house. Don always worked at "cost plus 10 percent." Each week, he would work on the house and at the end of the week present his bill for materials used plus his 10 percent labor fee. This was the usual arrangement for normal building work.

Since Dr. Lancaster was busy practicing medicine, his nurse, Miss Winnie Kirkpatrick, and Daddy actually ended up supervising the whole project. Don would drop his bill off at the doctor's office. Then Miss Winnie would take the bill to Daddy at the bank. Daddy would look over the bill just to see what had been done that week, then cut Don a check from Dr. Lancaster's bank account. The check would be given to Miss Winnie, who would have it back at the office for Don to pick up for the following week.

The house, including the landscaping and paved driveway, was totally finished and paid for sometime early in my sixth-grade school year.

Things did not turn out for the Lancasters the way they had planned. About the time they moved into the new house, Dr. Lancaster had a serious heart attack. After recovery, he decided to go ahead and close his office and move into retirement. That worked well in theory but not in practice. Since he had built a general practice largely around house calls and personal relationships, his old patients did not understand the concept of "retirement." The phone at the Lancasters' house rang day and night. "Since you closed the office, I had to call you at home," was the gist of most of these phone calls. He tried to manage a partial practice until the second heart attack nearly killed him. It had to end.

The Lancasters had a family farm in Horseshoe in Henderson County. So the plan was to leave Waynesville and move there so he would not be killed by his patients. He told Miss Winnie to go see Daddy and find out how much he had spent on the entire house project. The rest of the instruction was to ask Daddy if he knew anyone who wanted to buy the new house for exactly what the Lancasters had in it.

Daddy couldn't believe his ears when Miss Winnie came with the news. He added up the total cost of the house—landscaping, driveway, and everything. It came to almost exactly twenty thousand and five hundred dollars.

"That's what he wants for it. Do you think you might know anyone who would like to buy it for that?" It was 1955.

When Daddy came home from work that day, my true belief is that he had already made the deal for the house. But he got all of us in the car, and we went out to look at the house. The Lancasters were very cordial and showed us all around. They explained that they would have to leave the washer and dryer and all of the kitchen appliances because the house in Horseshoe had all this already. There would be no charge for these new appliances; they just came with the deal. On the way home, we all agreed to the rigid savings plans it would take for our family to make the move to "the new house."

It was the end of the school year, and the move was made. We actually slept in the new house first on my birthday, June 1. This house was called "the new house" from then until the day it was sold following our mother's death forty-three years later. (When the house sold, I discovered that it was nearly thirteen hundred square feet. We had moved in thinking it to be the largest house we could imagine!)

At our Plott Creek house, we had had a washing machine but only outdoor clotheslines for drying the clothes. In the wintertime, the sheets and towels would freeze flat and stiff as boards. In fact, all of the clothes dried outdoors on the line came off very stiff. But at the new house, the Lancasters had left for us a General Electric washer and matching dryer. They were in the laundry room behind the garage, where the boiler for the hot-water furnace was also located.

Mama was not good at dealing with things she was not born with. So the idea of a clothes dryer totally confused her from the start. She would have preferred to ignore the dryer and hang the clothes outside the way she had always done, except that there was no clothesline at the new house. The dryer was going to have to be mastered.

Daddy, on the other hand, delighted in new things. He decided that the clothes dryer was going to be the finest invention we had ever experienced, and he was going to show all of us how easy it was to use. "It will dry our clothes while we eat supper," he proclaimed before one of our first evening meals at the new house.

He waited until it was essentially time for us to sit down to eat and then excused himself for "just a moment." In several moments, he returned to the kitchen to announce that the wet clothes from the washing machine had now been put into the dryer and would be dry in one hour, "just about in time for us to finish our dessert." We had no dessert.

I am sure that we lingered at the table more than usual to wait for the hour to pass and watch Daddy make his presentation to Mama. He kept looking at his watch until finally the required time had passed. He pushed back his chair and said, "Excuse me for just a moment," and disappeared from the kitchen into the garage toward the laundry room.

We waited and waited. It seemed like he was gone a very long time. Finally, we heard him coming back. When he came in the door, he had the longest and most distressed face imaginable. Something was terribly wrong. He had in one hand a bath towel and in the other a bedsheet. Neither was folded; they were just draped over his outstretched hands.

"I do not know what happened, Lucille. I did just what the instructions in the book said to do, but the dryer has ruined all of our clothes." He held out the soft towel and softer sheet. "See, all of our clothes are as limp as they can be. Look, this towel is so limp it would not even scrape the water off of you!"

He had never seen softly dried clothes from a clothes dryer and truly thought he had completely destroyed the laundry. It was very good to see Mama get a chance to laugh at him for once.

Moving to the new house was an adventure for all of us, and it was the first of two things that made my coming thirteenth year a most significant one. You see, behind the garage and parallel to the laundry room was another, almost hidden room. Mrs. Lancaster had told Mama that it was called "the maid's room," and it was where their housekeeper kept her personal belongings and rested when she was not working during the day. Since we had no housekeeper, it was simply another room that we could decide how to use. As soon as I saw it for the first time, I laid claim to this remote room as the perfect place for me to put all of my stuff. I begged for it as the perfect place to do my homework and school projects, and much to my surprise, my parents agreed that it could be mine. (They realized quickly that I would be out of the house with all my messes and far away from the rest of the family.) I nicknamed the room my "Private Scientific Laboratory."

This room had its own entrance from the laundry room. It was not large, maybe eight by twelve, but it had a toilet and a sink, lots of shelves, a small closet, and a space (probably where the housekeeper's daybed had been) that was perfect for a large table for homework and my laboratory center. Having this space that really was my own was the greatest initial gift that came with the new house.

The second wonderful thing happened that Christmas. After begging for several years in vain, I began to get the feeling that, since I had a place to use it, I was at last going to get the chemistry set that would surely make my life complete.

What I wanted was the largest-sized chemistry set made by the A. C. Gilbert Company. The A. C. Gilbert Advanced Chemistry Set had glass bottles of chemicals ranging from aluminum sulfate to zinc sulfate. Of course, I had no idea what these were or what I could do with them. I just wanted the set. Daddy apparently talked Mama into the idea, and when Christmas came there was the gigantic chemistry set under the tree with a home waiting for it in my Private Scientific Laboratory.

The chemistry set was in a beautiful metal box that opened in sections and had little divided shelves and compartments in it. It was simply beautiful to look at. There were test tubes, pipettes, and beakers of several sizes. There was a small balance scale and even an alcohol burner. There was a book with it that told about all kinds of experiments that could be done. I showed Mama and Daddy how neatly I had arranged it all on my work table and tried to convince them that it was a very educational present. I could not have been more thrilled by anything in this world.

Then it was Mama who made it even better. "Just wait until

your uncle Jim gets here. He is a real chemist, you know. I bet he knows all about this stuff, and he can show you how to be careful and safe with all of it."

What Mama thought and the reality of Uncle Jim's advice were to be two totally different and wonderful things.

Uncle Jim was married to Aunt Nancy, one of my mama's six younger sisters. They lived less than a hundred miles away in Morristown, Tennessee, where Uncle Jim worked for the American Enka Company in a plant at Lowland, Tennessee. Yes, he worked in chemistry. I assumed that since he was grown up and had a real job, Uncle Jim would be a functional adult. Only much later did I realize that he was only about thirty years old and as yet did not have children of his own who were old enough to ruin, so he was glad to work with me.

Later on Christmas afternoon, Aunt Nancy and Uncle Jim arrived, and the fun started. They were going to stay with us for three days, and their visit turned out to be the best gift of all.

"Donald got a chemistry set for Christmas." It was Mama who told him. "I thought you might want to take a look at it and show him how to use it safely."

While I was listening to her hopeful words, I could already see Uncle Jim slightly grinning at the prospect.

We headed out to my laboratory. I had made a large table out of a door on two high sawhorses, and Uncle Jim immediately complimented me on having "an adequate lab table." I showed him the A. C. Gilbert Advanced Chemistry Set, and he was instantly impressed. He began to pick up the glass bottles and read off the labels: "Gum Arabic, Calcium Hydroxide, Powdered Iron, Copper Sulfate . . ." There were fifty-six bottles of chemicals in all. He was very impressed.

We spent the rest of that afternoon trying out little experiments that were described in the book. It seemed like Uncle Jim was having at least as much fun as I was. Once in a while, he would mutter to himself, "I wonder what this does?" when we tried an experiment.

We were really having a good time when Mama came out from

the garage to see what we were doing. "I hope you are being safe," was her expressed greeting.

Uncle Jim seemed to understand her completely. "Everything here is very educational, Lucille. Maybe we should show you something so you will see how much Donald is going to learn with this. Do you have any steel wool and vinegar in the kitchen? You see, almost everything you use in your house has something to do with chemistry."

Mama disappeared for a few moments and returned with a steel-wool pad and a bottle of apple cider vinegar.

"Now," Uncle Jim instructed, "hold the steel wool in your hand over the sink while I pour a little bit of vinegar on it. No, it won't hurt."

As Mama held the steel wool, he slowly poured vinegar evenly all over the pad, soaking it until the excess was running down into the sink.

"Now, tell us what you feel."

"It's getting warm all on its own! Yes, it's getting warm."

"Here's what's happening. The steel wool has a coating on it when it comes from the store so it won't rust. The acid in the vinegar takes off that coating, and as soon as oxygen hits the steel wool it starts to rust. Rust, or oxidation, is a chemical reaction, and like many chemical reactions it produces heat. So you are holding a chemistry experiment right in your hand. Isn't that educational?"

Mama guessed that it was. The good thing was that she was convinced we were being safe, and so she left us alone after that.

The next morning at breakfast, Uncle Jim had new ideas. "I was thinking in the night. There are some more chemical supplies that you can get without having to order them. After a while when the stores open, let's go to town, and I can show you about where you can find some things and what they are."

Daddy thought this was a great idea. Mama was not sure. But since Daddy wanted to go with us, too, and pay for whatever we got, he ruled the day.

About ten o'clock, we left for town. First, we went to the Farmers'

Christmas morning at our new house, 1958

Co-op. There, we found the veterinary medicine aisle for farm animals, and Uncle Jim picked out sulfur, carbon tetrachloride, and potassium nitrate (it was called "saltpeter" at the store, but the bag said it was potassium nitrate).

After that, we went to the drugstore. In the household cleaning department, we found Red Devil lye and muriatic acid. Over the counter from the pharmacist, we could buy chloroform, hydrochloric acid, silver nitrate, and sodium hydroxide. In the hair-care aisle, we bought hydrogen peroxide. I had no idea what all these things were for, but Uncle Jim seemed to know and wanted to stock up on all of them.

Back at home, we went all through the kitchen gathering things while Mama was in another part of the house. We took the vinegar and the baking soda and a box of salt. "We're in good shape now!" Uncle Jim said.

All afternoon, we hunted for small jars and bottles and carefully stored and labeled all the things we had bought on the trip to town. While this was very interesting, I was slightly afraid that Uncle Jim was on the verge of thinking the chemistry set was his Christmas present. I didn't need to worry, though, as the day after that, he and Aunt Nancy decided it was time for them to go home.

We were fairly regular visitors with Aunt Nancy and Uncle Jim. We could go over through Spring Creek to Hot Springs and be at their house in Morristown in about two and a half hours. About every other time, we would go over there, with them coming to our house the in-between times. As the new year rolled along, each time we saw them, Uncle Jim had something else for me that he had brought home from work at the American Enka laboratory.

At the same time, I was saving allowance and work money and ordering supplies. Before long, I had an actual Bunsen burner that had an LP gas tank like a gas grill to operate it. This was a great advancement over the small alcohol burner that had come with the original chemistry set. As the year went on, I assembled quite a collection of test tubes and racks to hold them, various Pyrex beakers and tubes of different shapes and sizes, pipettes and rubber tubes and stoppers. Soon, I had charcoal blocks and a real mortar and pestle.

Very often at the end of one of their visits, he would tell me about something I should try to find before the next time they came to our house. It would be what we needed for a new kind of experiment he had thought of. After one such visit, the instructions were specific and clear. "What I want you to do before next time is this: Save up all of the old aluminum foil that your mother has finished with. Wad it up in little balls and put all of them in a paper grocery bag. At the same time, see how many plastic dry-cleaning bags you can save up. Try not to punch any holes in them. We need them as solid as they can be."

For the next weeks, my mama had never used so much aluminum foil! I had a great supply in no time. The dry-cleaning bags were still easier. When clothes came back from Bill Dover's Cleaners, my parents never took the plastic bags off until they wore the clothes. The closet was full of perfect plastic bags. I was ready and waiting for the next time Uncle Jim came back.

There was only one thing wrong with my scientific laboratory. It was called "the Smiths." The Smiths were the neighbors who shared our driveway to the top of the hill, and they were old. They were so old that they lived in a world in which color had not yet been invented. Everything in their world was a sepia brown color, including their personalities. Their grass was brown, their car was brown, their dog was brown, even their house itself was a reddish brown. Mr. Smith always wore brown suits and brown hats. I am sure that they both had brown eyes.

The problem was that Mr. Smith's hobby was complaining to my daddy about me. Everything that went wrong in the entire neighborhood was certainly, in his version of things, my fault for being patently stupid. If I accidently rode my bike through some of Mrs. Smith's brown flowers, it was my fault. If I happened to push my brother too hard in the wagon and he ended up crying in their driveway, it was my fault. I think that even bad weather conditions he thought to be my fault. Now, with the scientific laboratory in full operation, I was sure that there would be more blame than ever on its way from the Smiths' house.

It was nearly a month later when Uncle Jim came back. He seemed as ready as I was to get on with the next big experiment, whatever it was. I proudly showed him the grocery bag now filled with aluminum foil balls and a good dozen plastic laundry bags. He told me I had done a perfect job. Then we got to work.

"We need a gallon glass jug, one with a small neck at the top where we can be in control of what goes into it and what comes out," Uncle Jim said.

This was easy. My daddy and Mr. Leatherwood made apple cider each fall of the year, and we had loads of gallon glass jugs they used for the cider. One would easily be contributed, and no one would be the wiser about it.

As soon as I came back with the jug, I learned that we were going to use the Red Devil lye that we had bought at the drugstore. We washed the big jug out very well. Uncle Jim said we needed to wash containers even if they looked clear because we could never tell what might be left in them. Once the washing was done, he carefully emptied the lye into the glass container, using a funnel from the chemistry-set supplies. Then he filled it about three-fourths full of warm water and stirred the mixture with a long glass rod he had brought to me several weeks earlier.

"This is a strong mixture of lye water," he warned. "We have to be very careful not to spill any of it or get it on our skin. Having it in this glass jug makes it a lot safer to handle. Now, let's get the dry-cleaning bags and get them all ready."

I brought out the dry-cleaning bags, and we proceeded to lay them out on the work table one at a time to check them for any holes or tears. If we found even the smallest hole, Uncle Jim would patch it carefully with a little piece of silver tape he called "duck tape." He had brought two rolls of the stuff, and what we did not use right now became a permanent part of our laboratory supply stash. After checking each bag for holes, we used the same tape to securely seal the holes at the top of the bags where the clothes hangers had originally come through.

When all this was done, we took everything outside in order to work on the paved driveway, where we had an outdoor surface that was level. This included the lye water, the aluminum foil balls, the plastic dry-cleaning bags, and a ball of cotton twine, from which he had cut about a foot-long string for each of the bags we were going to use.

Once outside, we spread everything on the driveway, and he got ready to tell me what to do.

"Get about a good double handful of those aluminum foil balls and drop them in this first bag." He held the bag open for me as I dropped in the requested amount. "Now, watch this carefully." He took the open end of the bag and scrunched it up together until he had only an opening left the size of the neck on the lye water jug. This opening went over the neck of the jug and was held tightly to keep any air or anything else from leaking. "Now, this should be fun. Pick up the other end of this bag and lift it up so that the aluminum foil falls down out of the bag and into the lye water. I'll hold it tight while you do it."

I carefully raised my end of the bag, and when the aluminum foil hit the lye water, it went crazy! It was like a mad, boiling reaction that was bubbling as hard as it could, and as it bubbled the plastic bag began to inflate. Uncle Jim held the bag in place until it was so full it was trying to take off. Then he took it loose from the jug, twisted the open end, and tied one of the pieces of string there to hold it closed. He let the bag loose. It jumped about ten feet into the air, then settled to an even rise as the prevailing wind carried it from southwest to northeast, out of our yard and right over the Smiths' house. We watched it with excitement until it finally disappeared from our sight.

"See? We just launched our first weather balloon!"

We laughed and hollered so much that both Daddy and Mama came outside to see what we were doing. We couldn't wait to show them.

The second dry-cleaning bag was prepared, filled, and launched. Mama and Daddy acted like they had never seen such a thing in their lives, and they hadn't!

"What is it?" Daddy asked.

"It looks dangerous!" Mama's reaction was totally predictable.

"It's not dangerous if you do things carefully, and that's what we're learning to do." Uncle Jim saved the moment. "We've just made ourselves a hydrogen gas generator, and we are launching weather balloons."

They watched while we filled and let go of number three.

"What are you learning about the weather from these?" Mama looked doubtful.

I stayed quiet as Uncle Jim took over. "We have learned that the wind today is from the southwest to the northeast, because that is the direction the airflow took each of our balloons. We learned that the visibility today seems to be unlimited, because we could see the balloons until they were so small they vanished, and not because our vision was limited by fog or clouds or smoke. And we learned about rain."

Mama was ready. "What did you learn about rain?"

"We learned that it's not raining today, or we would be waiting for another day to be out here doing this."

We all laughed. They stayed and watched us launch another balloon, then went back inside and left us to our own devices.

When all the balloons were gone, there was still a lot of the lye water left and we still had about a third of the aluminum foil balls I had collected.

"Let's put the lid on this jug and save the rest of the lye water," Uncle Jim said. "You may want to do this some more on your own after I am gone. But if you do, remember this: be very careful because this hydrogen gas is explosive."

And it was!

By the following Saturday, I had collected more aluminum foil and more dry-cleaning bags. It was a day when Mama and Daddy took Joe with them and went to Asheville. They asked me to go, but I told them I had some homework I needed to do (true!). So I was alone for the day.

It was when I launched the very first of the plastic-bag balloons that I got the idea. The string that had tied it closed at the bottom hung down like a little tail—or did it look like a little fuse? It would be wise to tie on a longer string, but it would be interesting to see just how explosive the hydrogen gas really was.

With the second balloon, I found out. I tied it shut with a longer string and just before letting it go lit the end of the string. The balloon made it about a hundred feet up into the air before it totally exploded with a huge bang. There was nothing visible left of it! Where did it go? It just exploded and totally disappeared. This was good! But maybe I needed to use even longer pieces of string.

Soon, I had the process perfected. If the string was too long, it would sometimes go out before burning up to the balloon, and the balloon simply flew away until it disappeared from sight. But if it was just long enough, the balloon would go several hundred feet up into the air before exploding and sometimes would actually have drifted way over the Smiths' house before it went off.

I still had three more dry-cleaning bags to go when it happened. I had been very careful to patch any holes and tears with the duck tape, but I must have missed a leak or two in the next balloon. It seemed to fill perfectly and was tugging to be set free when I lighted the string and let it go. But there was some hesitation as it rose into the air, and then it just stopped rising. There had to be a leak. There it went, drifting on the light air current, straight toward the tops of the white pine trees that separated our yard from the Smiths' house.

The Smiths had a little brown beagle-like dog named Snooper. Snooper lived in a doghouse that was down the hill just at the east edge of their yard. He was the world's slowest dog. Snooper had a little chain that kept him collared within a twenty-foot radius of the doghouse. Right against the back of the doghouse, Mr. Smith had two beehives of honeybees. Snooper didn't have enough energy to annoy the bees, and they left one another alone. Neighborhood cats knew all about Snooper and had no fear of him at all. In fact, they seemed to like to wander past, just out of reach of the end of his dog chain, and give him a little bit of bother.

I gave no thought at all to several things. It did not occur to me that the leaking balloon was headed directly toward Snooper's beehive-backed doghouse. Neither did it occur to me that on a Saturday the Smiths were at home watching black-and-white television in their living room. No, I simply watched the dry-cleaning-bag balloon barely clear the white pine trees and go sinking out of my sight, until the string fuse burned far enough and there was a tremendous bang as the hydrogen exploded.

From where I was, I could not see that the explosion had occurred as the balloon touched Snooper's doghouse. Apparently, the world's slowest dog set a new acceleration record as he shot out of the doghouse. When the twenty-foot chain ran out, he was moving so fast that he jerked the doghouse off its foundation. This resulted in both beehives falling over and scattering themselves over the ground as the bees swarmed from the hives. Inside, the Smiths were startled by the explosion and went running outside and right into the swarm of unhappy bees, which were glad to have something in addition to Snooper to sting.

And when everything was over, Mr. Smith somehow thought that the entire thing was my fault. Why, I didn't even know that the bag had a leak in it! And Daddy really thought that the entire thing was funny. His only comment on hearing all about it later was, "I just wish that I had been there!"

Now, my scientific laboratory was really in full swing. I didn't need to depend on Uncle Jim a lot anymore, but I still loved to be able to learn new things from him each time he came for a visit.

On an early-summer visit, we made a trip to town to replenish supplies. We got back and carefully labeled and put everything away and tried out a couple of mild experiments. I had been collecting rocks and minerals all this year, and he showed me how you could sometimes identify things by grinding a bit in the mortar and pestle and then placing it on a charcoal block and heating it with a blowpipe. Learning to use my cheeks to keep the blow-pipe airstream constant was something I loved to practice. I also thought it benefited my junior-high trumpet playing.

At the end of that visit, he had some words of advice for me. "Now, son, you know that we have tried a lot of experiments, but we never try something when I am not pretty sure what is going to happen. When I am gone, I don't want you to just randomly put things together. That could really be unsafe. Here's a good example." He pointed to the supplies we had just labeled and put in order from the day's shopping trip. "Look at what we bought today: sulfur and potassium nitrate. Why, that right there is part of what it takes to make gunpowder. Don't just play with it!"

I took this as a serious assignment. I would not just play with it. I would learn what other ingredients were required for making gunpowder and see if he was right.

We had a very old set of the *World Book Encyclopedia*, and it was the best reference thing in the house without going to the library. I looked up gunpowder and got all the information I needed. It said that gunpowder was a fast-burning propellant that, if confined, served as an explosive source of energy in firearms. It also told me that gunpowder was fairly simple. It was made of just three things: sulfur, charcoal, and saltpeter (in parentheses, "potassium nitrate").

It was an experiment waiting to be tried.

I had the potassium nitrate and the sulfur from our shopping trip to the Farmers' Co-op. And we had charcoal briquettes. All I needed to do was take a charcoal briquette and grind it into powder in my own mortar and pestle, and all three ingredients would be powdered and ready to mix.

The encyclopedia article said nothing about proportions, but even on my first try I discovered that exact proportions were not crucial, as long as I had all three of them well mixed together. There was no actual explosion, since it had to be properly confined to explode, but it burned furiously (and very noisily, I discovered). As it burned, it roared and threw off little burning sparks that I assumed to be sulfur, since it had a strong sulfuric smell. It was a very successful experiment from the start. I made quite a bit of the stuff in the coming days and began to try various applications with it.

By the time Uncle Jim came for the next visit, I was ready to show him what I had discovered. I had made a pretty good quantity of the homemade gunpowder and had filled a large-sized glass Coca-Cola bottle with the stuff. I took Uncle Jim with me, and we went down on the hillside away from the house—"for safety," as I said to him. He smiled and looked back to see that we were well out of sight from the house.

The bottle was buried in the ground right up to its neck and a thin line of the powder laid out from it for about twenty feet. "Watch this!"

Before he had time to suggest that we not try this, I had lit the line of powder, and in a couple of seconds the filled bottle ignited. It looked like a little jet engine or a fire geyser shooting up out of the ground. The roaring of the burning sound was wonderful, and as it burned it shot into the air eight or ten feet. Little burning globs of stuff shot all over everywhere, and it went on nearly half a minute before it was exhausted.

We both stood there and laughed out loud and watched the last remnants of smoke clear away.

"Let's dig up the bottle and see what it did to it." It was his suggestion.

We knew we had to wait for it to cool off, as even the ground around where it was buried was hot. After a little while, we dug out the bottle to discover that the heat had actually melted the glass into a distorted glob that had an interesting shape and had captured little bits of dirt, rocks, and sand in the process of doing this. We took it back to the house and washed off all the loose dirt. It was beautiful!

"Just look at this!" Uncle Jim proclaimed. "It's science and art at the same time. This really was an educational project!"

As we talked over what we had just observed, one of us remarked that the homemade powder looked like it might have propulsive possibilities, and this led to speculation about whether it could be used to build a rocket.

We tried that the very next day. A pipe became the body for the rocket. The hard part was trying to figure out how to attach the fins we had crafted from flattened tin cans. The big mistake was that we finally soldered them to the rocket body. When we tried to launch the rocket, it left the ground, but almost immediately the heat melted the solder and the fins fell off. With no guidance provided by the fins, we had a gunpowder-powered pipe wildly crashing around in the trees until it burned out and fell harmlessly to the ground. The biggest danger was that we could have set fire to the woods.

After that poorly planned experiment, we decided to give up on rocketry.

There is a sad part of the story that has to be told at this point. It would be better to leave this part out, but what comes later would not be understandable without it. So here we go: Mrs. Smith cleaned their entire house from top to bottom every day. (I think this is why it was colorless. She had long ago washed off all the color.) She even swept and mopped the paved driveway all the way down to the highway. People with out-of-town guests would often come over in the afternoon and drive up and down the highway to see if they could spot her and show their guests the woman who mopped the driveway.

The sad part: One day, she was up on a big A-frame ladder washing the windows. This had to be done very carefully, since they had been cleaned so often that the glass was now very thin. Without warning, she fell off the ladder and down into a concrete window well and fractured her skull. No one else was home, and by the time she was found she had been unconscious for some while. She lingered in the hospital for about two or three days and then died.

Shortly after her death, old Mr. Smith suddenly got a whole lot younger. He would come home from work and change into shorts and Hawaiian shirts. He started watering the yard until it actually turned green. He traded the old brown car for a brand-new baby-blue DeSoto that had huge tailfins in the back. He started wearing sunglasses that looked like mirrors you could see yourself in.

And he started having a lot of company, none of it male! It was what my daddy called "the Casserole Brigade." Every unmarried or widowed woman in town of "a certain age" began to wear a trail to his house, bringing him food. It was nonstop. He could have fed several families of neighbors off the food they brought him, and many of them seemed to stay quite awhile after the deliveries were made. Daddy said, "I think they want to ask him how he likes his new car."

This had gone on for several weeks, maybe more, when one day Mr. Smith came up to our house to talk with Daddy. I was out in the yard at the time and could not keep from hearing the conversation. "Joe," he started, "you will not believe what has happened. I can hardly believe it myself, and I'm the one it's happened to. I wanted to tell you about it first, since you might notice things happening around the house."

"Well, John, what is it? Are you going to tell me or just stand there? You look awfully happy."

Mr. Smith blushed. "I have a girlfriend."

"You do?" Daddy was astonished. "Where did you get her?"

"She came to the door. She is a wonderful cook. She makes the best tuna-noodle casserole ever. It has slivered almonds in it. And she makes wonderful banana pudding."

"Who is she, John? What's her name?"

Mr. Smith paused for a moment. Then he answered, "Her name is Goldie."

Daddy was puzzled. "Goldie who? I don't believe I know a Goldie."

Mr. Smith seemed to be trying hard to think. Then he said, "Just Goldie."

By then, Mama had arrived and was listening to the entire exchange. She immediately invited Mr. Smith to come and bring "Goldie Goldie" to our house for supper a week from Thursday.

She told us later it was so we could quietly interview her, in case she turned out to be a potential new member of the neighborhood.

That weekend, Mama and Daddy were gone with Joe all day on Saturday, so I had the entire day in the laboratory to myself. I had been thinking about how the homemade powder had so much propulsive energy, and that there must be some way to use it. We had happened to be watching television one night, and there was a news feature about land-speed trials at the Bonneville Salt Flats in Utah. It was very interesting and, it turned out, very educational. I did not know that the "cars" in the land-speed trials were not powered by internal combustion engines, but rather by jet engines. They went so very fast that some of them even ran straddling a kind of track or rail to keep them straight at high speeds. I both thought and dreamed about that, and with a full Saturday in the laboratory began to try out an idea: what if I could make a little car that was propelled by homemade gunpowder?

First thing was a body. This was fairly easy. I simply took a remnant of plywood that had a sort of swept-back triangular shape and decided it would do. The wide V shape already gave it at least the appearance of being aerodynamic. After that came wheels. I don't think my brother, Joe, ever did figure out what happened to the undercarriage and wheels from his fire truck. The real trick, though, was going to be the engine—or, as I decided, the engines. Of course, it should be twin-engined, and that was not as hard as it seemed. I had accumulated a fair bit of copper tubing in my laboratory supplies. It was easy to bend to any shape and came in several diameters, the largest of which had a full one-inch opening. I turned the "car" upside down and laid it on its top on the work table. Then it was not too hard to carefully bend a piece of the copper tubing in a U shape, so that both open ends of the tubing came out the back just on either side of the double wheels. I sawed the length off until it was just right, then fastened it to the bottom of the car with wires twisted through holes drilled in the plywood.

Looking at the creation, it seemed to me that the mechanics of the car were complete, but it needed to be beautified a little bit on the top side. Seeing the shape of the triangular car reminded me of a childhood book I had loved that was all about airplanes. In the book, the most fascinating picture of all was of what was called "an experimental flying wing." In this picture, the entire aircraft looked like a big, thick wing, inside which was all the space for passengers and cargo. I don't think it was actually ever built, but it was very interesting to me. This became my visual model for the top shape of the car.

I glued several thin strips of balsa wood along the front edge of the "wing" and sanded them round on the leading edge. Then I took cheesecloth that I had from my model-airplane days and glued it from that front edge back in a slant to meet the rear edge of the wing. Since I had been building models for years, I had plenty of dope, glue, and paint to coat the cloth until it was totally stiff. After that, I made a little place for the invisible driver to sit by gluing the windshield from a broken model car to the front of the V. After a few coats of red paint edged by some silver pinstriping, I had a creation I could hardly wait to try out.

It had taken the entire day to do this, and I was extremely proud of my work, but it would now have to be put away for a while.

The following Thursday, we were all excited. This was the day we were going to get to meet Mr. Smith's new girlfriend and see what a "Goldie Goldie" looked like. It was summertime, so there was no school for any of us; we could get ready all day. Mama cooked an eye of round roast with plenty of gravy for her mashed potatoes. She also made a squash casserole with squash from our garden. We had lots of fresh tomatoes and fried okra from the garden and finished everything off with a big coconut cake. Joe and I wondered all day about what someone called Goldie would look like. Daddy came home from work early, and we all set up our watch stations at various front windows, where we could look toward the white pines that separated our yard from Mr. Smith's.

It was right on six o'clock. We could hear them coming before we could see them. Goldie Goldie was wearing a pair of long, dangling earrings that could have been recycled from the percussion section of the Chicago Symphony.

As Goldie came through the pine trees, the first thing Mama noticed was the bright, brassy color of her long hair. "Well," Mama huffed, "I see now where she got her name. It didn't come from her grandmother. I think it came from aisle number two at Curtis's Drug Store."

It was Daddy's turn to comment. "Lucille, look at how short she is. Why, as short as she is, it looks like she could have found a dress that would come down farther on her."

We were all watching. Goldie was walking in bare stocking feet and carrying a pair of red shoes with five-inch spike heels that nobody could have possibly walked in. She was ready to put them on just before they rang the doorbell at our house.

We welcomed them in and very soon sat down at the table to eat. Conversation started, but pretty soon Goldie Goldie had used up all of her words. After that, Daddy and Mr. Smith had to carry on the whole conversation themselves. Gradually, they were talking about things I had never even heard of in my life.

"John," Daddy started, "do you know why we picked this house out and bought it to start with?" I thought it was because we got such a good deal when the Lancasters had to move away, but I listened to see if Daddy had other reasons to tell about.

Mr. Smith replied, "No, Joe. I guessed it was just because you wanted to live next to me as your neighbor."

"Of course, that was part of it," Daddy recovered. "But there was another reason: it was that big, flat hilltop front lawn with that ring of trees surrounding it. You see, when I was a boy, the automobile had just been invented. I never even saw an automobile until I was five or six years old. Then, before you could turn around, everybody and his brother had cars. Now, listen! About the time we were looking for a new house, the helicopter came out. I thought it was going to be just like it was with automobiles, and in no time everybody would have their own helicopter. When I saw that big, flat hilltop front lawn, I just knew it would be the perfect place to land my helicopter!"

All at once, Goldie broke in: "Or a UFO!"

Mama laughed out loud, and the course of the entire evening changed in an instant.

Goldie Goldie got her words back! "That is not funny!" she burst out. "I have been on one!"

All conversation and all eating immediately stopped as we waited to hear.

"It was one evening after work when I was up at my trailer fixing supper. I heard a great big noise outside that sounded like four or five locomotive freight trains up in the sky. When I ran out in the yard and looked up, there that thing was, a-whirling and a-shooting fire in every direction and spinning around and around in the sky. If anybody tells you that they is round, they have never seen one. It was like a big triangle of a thing with fire a-coming out all around the edges. It circled down to the ground and made a big hole about twenty-seven feet deep as it was a-landing right there behind my green trailer. Before I could run in the house, those little things come a-running out of it and grabbed me. They had heads like big, giant brains and great big green eyes that stood out on stalks so they could turn every which direction. They dragged me down in that spaceship and took off up into outer space. Out there, they put me to sleep and drained all of the blood out of me and put some kind of other stuff back in my veins and arteries. And when they let me out, I'll tell you, I have not been the same since."

Mama leaned over to Daddy and whispered, "I wonder what she was like before that?"

Supper seemed to come to an end very quickly after that, and Mr. Smith soon excused the two of them and took Goldie back home with him.

The very next day, he came walking up in our yard to talk with Daddy. He looked very distraught. "Joe," he said, "I didn't know."

"You didn't know what, John?"

"Anything." It was a sad answer. "I had no idea that the woman was just flat out looney. No idea."

Daddy asked, "Where did you say that you got her?"

"She came to the door. She brought food. She is actually still a wonderful cook. But she is going to embarrass the life out of me if people get to meet her. I don't know how, but I need badly to get rid of her. What can I do, do you think?"

Daddy had a bright idea. "Why don't you lock her out?"

"I tried that. It kept her out of the house, but I came home late one day and she had started charcoal in the grill down on the hill and was already cooking steaks. As soon as the smell hit me in the nose, my brain went into disorder, and I just let her back in. I don't know what I am going to do. I'll tell you, I would give a hundred dollars never to see that woman again."

With that, Mr. Smith started on what looked like a very sad walk back home.

Back in the laboratory, the gunpowder-powered car was ready to try out. I was proud of it, but I had encountered one little problem that I hoped to be able to solve. When I filled the copper tube with my homemade propulsive powder and then put the car down on its wheels, a whole lot of the powder fell out of the tubing. How was I going to manage to light up the engines if I couldn't solve this little glitch?

After thinking about it and studying the car for a long while, I got an idea. I found the box I was looking for in the garage closet. From the box, I picked out two flat washers that would barely slip inside the open ends of the tube. The solution was to place the flat washers just inside the ends of the copper tubes, them crimp down on them hard with Channellock pliers.

The washers were now installed where they would hold the gunpowder more securely in place—and, what I did not yet know, increase the propulsion immensely by simulating rocket restrictor valves. When I now looked at the way the front edge was shaped like a big wing, I wondered if my creation might even take to the air when I got to try it out.

There was one more step to perfection. I remembered that, when watching the Bonneville speed-trial program, I had seen how the jet-powered cars there ran on a control track or rail that kept them straight. I decided to put a water hose out in the sun until it got soft so I could straighten it out real well. Then I would lay the water hose in a straight line down the center of the driveway. I figured that if I put the car down on the water hose with the wheels on either side of it, the water hose would keep it in a straight line when it took off. All I needed now was to top off the engines, figure out a way to make fuses, and hope for a good, full day when nobody in the family was at home.

It took a couple of weeks for the ideal day to come. It was a Saturday when Mama and Daddy were going to help out at my grandmother's house. I lamented sorely that, being now in junior high, I had so much weekend homework that I could not go with them. They sympathized and wished me well at finishing all my work and, taking Joe with them, left me home alone on a beautiful, clear day. It was everything I had been hoping for.

They didn't actually leave until after lunchtime, so I had a lot of nervous waiting to do. I used this time to do the actual homework I did have, partly for show for the family and partly so that it would indeed be all out of the way when clear laboratory time came. Finally, they were gone and I could get things under way.

When I got the car out, I realized that I had, in excitement, failed to check everything carefully. The engine tube was not fully loaded. A lot of propulsion powder had been spilled in adding the restrictor washers, so I had to spend time to make a fresh batch so there would be a full power charge. While doing that, I laid the water hose out in the sun so it would be totally pliable when needed later.

Once the engine tubing was loaded, I worked out the fuse issue. This was done by finding some thin tissue paper in the wrapping-paper stash, laying a line of powder along a crease folded into a narrow strip of it, then twisting the paper around the powder line very tightly. I made two of these and inserted one end of each into the open washer ends of the two engines. After that, I twisted the dangling fuses together so that they could both be lighted at the same time with a single match. Things were almost ready.

Before taking the car outside, I went out and checked the hose. It was totally soft and ready. The rubber hose was then carefully and straightly laid right down the center of the paved driveway from the house toward the edge of the hill. The guidance system was in place.

Back in the laboratory, I picked up the car, the conjoined fuse dangling, and grabbed a big box of strike-anywhere matches from the table. Once outside, I placed the car carefully over the hose, and the wheels aligned so that one set was on each side of the hose.

My only regret was that I had no audience for the firing. I would have to appreciate my work alone.

Kneeling down, I struck the wooden match, touched it to the twisted end of the common fuse, and ran back inside the open door of the garage to watch. The fuse burned a little more slowly than I had anticipated; I think I had used a lot more tissue paper than was actually needed. In a short moment, I could see that it had burned far enough to have passed the joined section and now was burning on both separate ends toward the twin engines. What never occurred to me was that these two fuses might not burn at exactly the same rate. It was visually obvious that one engine side was going to ignite before the other.

Then, suddenly, it happened. One fuse reached the big load of powder, and that side ignited full force all at once. As the car took off, the other fuse dropped loose, so the second side would never ignite. The entire load of gunpowder would be burning unevenly from one side.

As the car gained speed in a great hurry, I was glad that I had used the hose to keep it on a straight track. Since one side was spewing out all of the burning powder, the car was trying to make a left turn, and would have except that the hose kept it from losing direction.

All of a sudden, it left the ground. The wing-shaped car leapt skyward in a bound, now spinning to the left as the one engine took complete control. The last thing I could see clearly was the now-flying thing going right over the top of the white pine trees on its own course directly toward Mr. Smith's house. As I watched in approving amazement, the whirling car was spurting fire and globs of burning, smoking sulfur all over that part of the sky.

I had no idea at all that on this Saturday Mr. Smith was not presently at home. Nor did I know that Goldie Goldie had arrived there and, locked out of the house, already had the charcoal started in preparation for cooking the steaks for their Saturday night. I didn't know any of this until I heard her desperate screaming as she heard and saw the spinning triangular demon descending straight toward her. "They're coming back! They're coming back!"

Her screams apparently terrified Snooper, who came out of his doghouse with a terrific howl and once again jerked over the now-repaired beehives. The dog's howls and the jerked-over beehives completed Goldie's terror, and she broke into a screaming run out of Mr. Smith's yard and down the back side of the hill through Owen Janes's cow pasture.

When Mr. Smith got home after that, he found a confusing scene. There was Goldie Goldie's Ford abandoned in the driveway. There was an overturned charcoal grill with burning charcoal scattered all over the ground, smoking in the grass. There was Snooper, enjoying a section of lawn that had not previously belonged to him and eating two excellent raw steaks that had lost their destination. The bees were gone. They had more sense than to stay after all of this. The last thing he saw was the still-burning remains of what he immediately knew had to have come from my scientific laboratory. I was at the same time nowhere to be found.

It didn't take long for him to put together what had happened, especially since she never came back to get her car. After three or four days, he called Fred Campbell, the sheriff, and asked him to come and run the plates on the car and get it towed back to wherever she lived in her green trailer. None of us ever saw Goldie Goldie again.

That is the end of the story, except for one thing. A couple of days after that, Daddy came home from the bank with a huge smile on his face. He winked at me, then gave me a little jerk of his head that said, *Come with me. I want you to see this.*

We went inside to where Mama almost had supper on the table. As usual, he gave her a little "I'm home!" kiss and waited for the question she could always be counted on to ask: "Well, Joe, did anything interesting happen at work today?"

Daddy was smiling at me so that she could not see his face. "Oh, it was a pretty normal day, nothing much out of the ordinary. But there was one unusual thing that I do not quite understand."

"What was that?" She fell right into his trap.

"Well," he spoke slowly, "our neighbor Mr. John Smith came in the bank this afternoon, and with no explanation in the world he put a hundred dollars in Donald's savings account."

Punishment

The oldest relative I knew in childhood was Daddy's half-brother, my uncle Grover. He was the relative who lived closest to us, hardly more than a mile away, and the one whom we saw more often than any other. A lawyer in town, he had an office directly behind the bank where Daddy worked, and the courthouse was straight across Depot Street from the bank. Daddy saw him almost every day. In addition, he and Aunt Jessie also went to the Methodist church, so we were with them again every Sunday.

While I knew that he was much older than Daddy and the other uncles, I did not really know what "half-brother" meant until I was much older. All I knew was that he was another uncle, but one who was different, in that Daddy treated him in an extra-respectful way.

Uncle Grover and his sister, my aunt Flora, were the two surviving children of Granddaddy Davis's first family. He was born on New Year's Day in 1885, between the election and inauguration of

Grover Cleveland as president. Granddaddy had insisted on naming him for the new president, perhaps a prelude to his own later political career.

I knew that Daddy always called him "Mr. Grover," not yet knowing that he had in fact been Daddy's first schoolteacher. In his first incarnation, Uncle Grover had been a schoolteacher in a one-room schoolhouse in which half of his sixteen students had been his own half-brothers and half-sisters. He taught school for several years while he was reading law in preparation for taking the North Carolina Bar examination.

Uncle Moody, Uncle Harry, Daddy, and Uncle Frank, as well as their sisters, Mary, Esther, and Ruth, had been students of their half-brother, Grover. He was, when teaching school, not yet married and still living at home with all of them. The story was that each morning he would make all of his siblings wait at home until he had walked out of sight toward school before they could leave behind him. That way, none of the other students would see them walking to school together, and he would maintain his status as teacher and keep them from being embarrassed by his attention. In the afternoon, they returned home in the opposite order; the children left school first, and he followed later.

Daddy once told me that on the first day of each school year "Mr. Grover" would have a talk with the students about seriousness and discipline. He told them that his rule was that "you plan your work, then you work your plan." Planning was very important to him. He saw report cards as the evaluation of what kind of life a student was already planning. Those who made good grades were planning a good life, while those who were failing were already showing the kind of adult life they were planning.

On that same first day of school, after the little talk, he had the students go outside to a big hickory tree that grew at the edge of the woods. There, he directed them each to cut a hickory limb as long as they were tall. They were then each to carve their initials on their own personal limb (every student carried a pocketknife in those days, as they might need it to sharpen pencils or writing quills) and stand it in the front corner of the schoolroom where they could see it as they faced the front of the room. Daddy said that Mr. Grover never had to pick up one of the limbs or use it for punishment, but the students saw that he had a clear and defined plan and knew that he would "work his plan" if they were out of order. More than any other relative, it was Uncle Grover who taught me that the secret of future success is planning in the present. He was the one who taught me that logistics always have priority over tactics.

There were many small family stories about those days in school with an older brother as teacher. The most memorable was an often-told story about Uncle Frank and Uncle Harry having rabbit traps when they were about eight and twelve years old. They checked their rabbit traps and discovered one day that they had caught a feral tomcat. It was the fall of the year, and they knew that there would be no fire in the potbellied stove at school in the warm afternoon, but that Mr. Grover would need to build a fire to warm up the school early the next morning. So they took the wild cat to the school and deposited it in the potbellied stove for the night. The next morning, Mr. Grover came to school early to start the fire and get things ready. When he opened the door of the stove, the angry trapped cat came out clawing right in his face, and school was out for the day! It was not until adulthood that either of these boys admitted how the cat had gotten into the stove.

While teaching school, Uncle Grover read law at nights and on weekends under the supervision of a lawyer named Haynes there in Haywood County. After lawyer Haynes decided that Uncle Grover was ready, with no degree of any kind, it was time for him to take the bar exam. The exam was completed, and the result showed that Uncle Grover had made a perfect score on constitutional law and had missed only one question on civil and criminal law. He once told me that he wished it had been the other way around. In more than fifty years of practicing law, "I never had a case involving constitutional law," he said. "If I had to miss a question on the exam, I wish it had been on that part!" He was always thinking about the connection between planning and performance.

I gradually learned about the esteem in which my own uncle Grover was held by residents of Haywood County. After he passed the bar, he became the solicitor, now called the district attorney, for the seven westernmost counties in North Carolina. He traveled the district and prosecuted cases in each of the seven county seats. He was known never to carry anything with him into the courtroom. He was simply mentally prepared and held in memory all that he needed to know for each day in court.

Throughout childhood, I heard repeatedly several stories about Uncle Grover as a young lawyer. The first one he often told on himself. One day, he was traveling to Franklin, North Carolina, to try cases in district court in Macon County. He was early in his career and could afford to drive only a Model T Ford. As he traveled from Dillsboro up over Cowee Mountain, the transmission bands on the Model T proved to be so worn that the old car would not pull over the top of the mountain. Since reverse gear was used much less and those transmission bands were not so worn, he tried backing over the top. This did not work either, and he sat there in the car trying to decide what he was going to do. The old road was unpaved, and there was no other traffic at all from which he might get a ride.

About that time, a man came along who was riding a mule toward Franklin. The man, never named in the story, stopped by the Model T and asked Grover if he needed some help. After the situation was explained, the man suggested that they tie the mule to the back of the car, and when Uncle Grover tried to go backwards again, the mule would help to pull him over the top. They did it, and it worked! The man would take no pay for his help. He just got back on his mule and resumed his travels, while Grover headed down the other side of Cowee as fast as he could to get to court on time.

As the day went along, one case after another was called, and the docket went forward. When everyone came back into court after the lunch break, the judge called the first afternoon case. It was a man who had been caught making illegal corn whiskey with a still hidden in a hole dug out under his barn. When the man came forward to sit at the defendant's table, it was the very man who had pulled Grover over the mountaintop with the mule.

Not knowing exactly what he was going to do, Uncle Grover told us that he listened as the judge began to question the man.

"Do you have a lawyer?" the judge asked.

"No, Your Honor. I reckon I am just going to have to represent myself. Couldn't afford no lawyer."

"Well," the judge went on, "do you have any character witnesses to speak on your behalf?"

"No, sir, Your Honor. I don't have no character witnesses," the man despaired.

The judge was trying to be fair as he could. He went on, "Well, sir, is there anyone here in this courtroom whom you know who might say something good in your behalf?"

The man looked around. A big smile came over his face. "Well, Your Honor, the only friend I have in this courtroom is the solicitor over there. He and I just spent part of the morning together."

With an amazed look on his face, the judge looked at Uncle Grover. "Well, Mr. Prosecutor, this is quite unusual. But I am going to ask you anyway. Can you say anything good about this gentleman who is seated at the other table from you?"

Uncle Grover looked up. "I do not know him very well, Your Honor, but he will help a fellow out in a time of need."

With that, the judge nol-prossed the case (decided not to take it further) and suggested that the man not be seen again similarly charged in his courtroom.

After several years of building his reputation as a prosecutor, Grover opened his little office behind the bank building in Waynesville. From that office, he continued to practice law for over sixty years, never having a partner, an assistant, or even a secretary. He handled everything from wills and deeds to capital murder cases.

During those early years of practice, Grover's house in town was the town home for anyone in the rest of the family who needed to go to Waynesville for any reason. He always had a milk cow, a garden, and a small tobacco allotment, even though he was right off Main Street within walking distance of his office.

At the same time, the younger half-brothers were finishing their own schooling. There was not yet a public high school near Iron Duff, so Moody and Harry were sent by their father, my grandfather, to the Cullowhee Institute, located on the top of the hill right in the middle of the present Western Carolina University campus. It was almost twenty-five miles to Cullowhee, so the boys roomed and boarded there while they were in school.

The school was run by Professor Reynolds, who gave his name to a dormitory later located where the school originally operated. He was a strict taskmaster with his all-male students. Even though he and his family had a home nearby, he himself always slept on a cot at the foot of the stairs of the dormitory to be sure that none of the boys slipped out at night.

There were great complaints from Harry and Moody about the paucity of the cuisine served to the students. Eventually, Harry came up with a plan to supplement their diet. He discovered that Professor Reynolds himself had a sizable flock of chickens in a lot behind his house. So, one night, he and a couple of friends slid down the gutter to keep from getting caught and raided the chicken lot. They caught a big, fat hen, wrung its neck, and skinned it (since they had no way to scald and pluck it). They then built a fire and boiled the chicken in an old coffeepot they had brought for that very purpose.

What they did not count on was the smell of the cooking chicken. Professor Reynolds was wakened from his guardian sleep by a wonderful odor, which he followed into the woods behind his house. There, he caught the three culprits just as they were polishing off the last of the purloined chicken.

The professor told the three boys that he knew it was his chicken they had stolen and eaten and that, unless they each paid him fifteen dollars for the loss, they would be kicked out of school with no credit and no refund. This meant that he was about to collect forty-five dollars for a 1915 chicken! Harry got mad, and before daylight he had walked to Sylva, then caught a train to Waynesville. There, he went to brother Grover's house to tell him what had happened.

Grover's solution was simple. He took Harry with him to his office and there typed, on his letterhead, a letter to Professor Reynolds from "Harry Davis's Attorney." It simply said that Harry Davis was preparing to sue Professor Reynolds for blackmail.

Once the letter was delivered, there was an immediate apology issued to Uncle Harry, and nothing else was ever said about the chicken. Harry also declared that the food improved considerably after that.

I grew up with these stories and with Uncle Grover's near presence in my life. He was nearly sixty when I was born and was forever the oldest person I intimately knew. It was a relationship of love, admiration, and a dose of respectful fear.

Daddy and Uncle Grover loved to do what they called "debating." (Mama called it "arguing.") When they had been in school, speech and debate were a mainstay part of the curriculum, and the addiction continued with them throughout life. After a Sunday dinner, for example, the two of them would sit at the dinner table and choose a topic for debate. Then they would go at it, sometimes for the afternoon. They didn't care which one of them took which side, they just liked the mental exercise of defending a point of view as long as possible. I loved to listen to these sessions.

The subjects varied: Should we have mandatory fluoride added to the public water system? Who has been treated more poorly, blacks or Indians? If Kennedy is elected, will the pope determine foreign policy? They could go on and on.

On one particular Sunday afternoon, it was Daddy who began the debate. "Mr. Grover," he started in politely, "I would like to submit to you that the law profession has gone soft on crime. It is not like in the good old days."

Never one to avoid a baited hook, Uncle Grover took a bite.

"Tell us all what you mean, Joe. I know you can't be right. Let's hear about it."

Daddy took off. "Just think about it. Back in the old days, a fellow would get up in the morning and decide that he was going to murder one of his friends. For the argument, the reason doesn't matter, he just needed to kill the man. So he gets his gun and goes out and shoots the man and kills him. As soon as the dead man hits the ground, everybody in the community knows who did it, so the sheriff goes out and rounds up the suspect and arrests him. By that afternoon, the judge has arrived, and they head over to the courthouse and get on with the trial. The witnesses are already there, and they give out the story, and in a little while the man is found guilty and sentenced to be hanged. Since everybody concerned is already assembled, they get the noose fixed up, and they hang the man at sundown. Now, that was real punishment."

Uncle Grover listened carefully. "Go on, Joe."

Daddy continued his argument. "Nowadays, it is so easy. A feller gets up in the morning and decides he needs to kill a friend of his. He goes on out and kills the man, and then it starts. They have to have a big investigation instead of just arresting the man who did it. Then they can't decide whether to arrest him or not. That part takes a few weeks. When they do arrest him, he gets bailed out while the grand jury decides whether he ought to go on trial. When they finally decide to try the man, months have passed.

"It takes a few more months before the trial date comes along, and when it finally starts, it lasts for several weeks. Then the jury has to deliberate for a few days. They finally find the man guilty, but they don't sentence him until another time period passes for the sentencing part of the trial.

"At last, they sentence the man to death, then they put him on death row, but they don't do it! He can linger around on death row for the rest of his natural life, and the sentence never is carried out. And that, Grover, is why I say that the law has gone soft on crime."

Uncle Grover smiled. This argument did not seem to be a

challenge to him at all. He started in. "Well, Joe, since you are not in the legal profession, you obviously do not understand the true nature of punishment. Let me explain it to you: the true nature of punishment is not physical, but mental. And we have just about perfected it."

Daddy looked puzzled. "I'm listening."

Uncle Grover went on. "Let's start with your 'old days.' Back then, a man would get up in the morning and decide to kill his neighbor. Before the morning was over, they had caught him and put him in jail to be tried for murder. Since there was no reason to wait, they got up a jury and two lawyers, sent for the judge, and got on with it that very afternoon. By three o'clock, the man had been tried and convicted and sentenced to death by hanging. At six o'clock that very same day, they hanged the man, and he was dead. From sentence to hanging, from three to six—that is exactly three hours of punishment, and then it was all over."

Daddy stared. He was trying to follow the argument.

"Today," Grover continued, "look at the progress. A feller gets up in the morning and decides to kill his neighbor. He knows all about modern science, so he starts worrying before he even does it about whether he is going to get caught or not. He changes his mind about six or seven times about how he is going to pull off the killing, and then he finally decides he is going to stab the man to death, so there won't be any gun to trace to the killing.

"So he stabs the other feller to death, and then he really starts to worry. 'Are they going to figure out that I am the one who did it? Are they going to catch me?' He about worries himself to death because it takes the law three full weeks to investigate the case and decide who the suspect is.

"So he is finally arrested and turned over to the grand jury. The grand jury is not going to meet for two months, so the murderer has two more months to worry about whether he is going to face trial or not. He can't sleep, and he can't eat. All he can do is worry. He would do about anything to get it over with. At last, the grand jury meets, and his worry compounds. 'Will they bind me over or not?' They do, and the trial is scheduled.

"It is four more months before the trial starts, and all he can do is worry. When it finally comes, the trial takes two weeks, and it is nonstop worry. 'Will they find me guilty or not?' He just about can't stand it. At last, the trial ends, and he has to worry and wait for three more days while the jury deliberates. By now, he is pulling his hair out and crying all night. He has lost thirty pounds. Then the verdict comes out: guilty. But what will the sentence be? Instead of finding out, he has to worry for two more weeks until the sentencing time comes. He develops ulcers and a heart condition from waiting and fretting.

"At last, the judge announces the sentence: he is sentenced to die in the gas chamber. But they don't do it! They put him down there in Central Prison, and a whole bunch of other lawyers get into it to be sure that he has more time to worry before he gets a chance to die and get out of all of it. The poor feller is begging to get it over with, but they won't do it.

"You see, Joe, worry is the main heart of punishment, and we just about now have it perfected."

I came to wish later that the two of them had never had that conversation. My daddy took it to heart: worry is the real heart of punishment. And he began to use it on me!

Up until this moment, whenever I committed what Daddy considered to be a "felony," there was immediate confrontation and immediate punishment. Even if the punishment happened to be corporal, it was over and mostly forgotten in less than an hour. After this so-called debate, whenever I committed a felonious act, Daddy would act like he didn't know I had done it. Even if he was present, he would pretend that he never even saw what happened.

That's when the worrying would start. I would begin to wonder, *Does he know? Maybe not. But if he knows, when is he going to say something about it?* I could come up with all kinds of reasons that the capture or confrontation was being put off: *People are watching. He is just going to wait until we are alone. He is thinking about it and trying to decide how he is going to kill me.* I could not deal with the fact that nothing was being done about what I had just done. The worry would begin to drive me crazy. I would actually come to the point of confession just to get it over with so life could go back to normal again.

Here is the whole story of one of those most memorable times.

During my entire Boy Scout career, I loved the camping trips more than any other troop activity. Getting away from home, hiking, going out into the woods, sleeping out, building fires, cooking over the fires—all these things were sublimely fulfilling to me as an early teenager.

My very best friends, David Morgan and Bill McInvaille, also loved camping and life in the woods, and this love bound us together more and more firmly.

In the eighth grade, I discovered that David's aunt Mary Jean's father, old Mr. Homer West, had a fox-hunting cabin way up on Big Stomp Mountain outside of town, and that he might allow David to take some of his best friends up there and go camping overnight. David invited me, and on the first trip Mr. West had us take him so he could show us all about it. He had a green Jeep, into which we loaded our food and other supplies, including two of his fox hounds with us in the back. He also carried with him a little lap dog that he could never leave behind. We had a great trip, and Mr. West allowed that we could now take the Jeep when we wanted to and go camping at the cabin as often as we could. This became our regular weekend adventure.

After one of the trips, we were talking to some of the girls who happened to be our classmates about our great camping adventures. We learned that they also loved to go to the woods and camp out as much as we did. After we exchanged experiences, we jokingly stated that it would be great educational fun if someday we might get to go on a camping trip together with them to share the wonders of nature. They laughed, also knowing that this was as impossible as raising a flying pig.

Our conversations about camping, however, went on through the next several years. We graduated from Boy Scouts to total

Mr. Homer West (who owned the Jeep and cabin), David Morgan, the author, and Bill McInvaille

camping on our own and discovered that the girls had graduated from Girl Scouts to planning their own woodland trips. It seems that, not having the cabin like we did, they usually camped in the woods below Amelia Gibson's house off Walker Road. Their parents allowed them to do this because they knew where they were and also knew that Amelia's parents (her mother was a school-teacher) would take care of them if bad weather or any other calamity occurred. Again we talked about how nice it would be if we ever got to go together, and again we laughed at the absurdity of such an idea.

Time continued to pass, and we eventually turned sixteen years old. In North Carolina, on the day of one's sixteenth birth-day, there are three things that almost always happen: you go to the Division of Motor Vehicles, you turn in your brain, and they give you a driver's license. When you are a sixteen-year-old with a new driver's license, you do not need a usable brain for quite a long time!

That time came, and in addition to driving the Jeep up on the mountain, we could now drive other vehicles on the highways in daylight hours. In the coming weeks, events conspired to create an idea that seemed to have great possibilities.

One Friday afternoon, we headed out to go to the cabin for a camping weekend. When we got out to Mr. West's house to load up in the Jeep, it would not start. At first, we thought we would have to walk up to the cabin and carry all of our gear, but David's uncle Don came out of the house and saw our dilemma. "Don't walk up there, boys. Take my pickup truck. Just throw your stuff in the back and go slowly." We discovered that day that the pickup truck could not only make the trip, we could carry a lot more in the back of the truck than we ever managed to get into the little Jeep.

I am never sure, in memory, who initially came up with the idea, but I do know that once it came up we spent most of the camping trip talking about it. The idea was that, with the pickup truck, we could put girls in the back and cover them up with a tarp and bring them to the cabin with us. The idea was thoroughly discussed and, we thought, perfected in brilliance. All we had to do was set the plan in motion.

We explained the idea to six girls. Our suggestion was that they tell their parents that they were going to go camping in Amelia Gibson's woods the following Friday night. It was important, though, that they not tell Amelia about this, as she did not need to know how she was being used. Then we would make a plan to pick each one of them up individually in a different place after school on Friday. They did not need to bring anything; we would bring all the food and the sleeping bags and everything else that was needed. We would take them up to the cabin, and at last we would get to have our dream camping trip together.

All six of them instantly agreed. The three of us boys thought this to be wonderful odds for us. We were too stupid to figure out that with six of them and three of us, if we tried anything untoward, they could just kill us.

All that week, our school days were filled with whispers and sly looks exchanged with those inside the big plan. This would surely be the finest weekend of our lives.

It was no problem for the three of us boys. We went to the cabin almost every Friday night, and nothing was unusual about that. All we had to do was be sure that David's uncle Don was willing for us to take the pickup truck. David told him we were building a refrigerator box to go into the spring behind the cabin and needed to haul our building supplies up there, and he agreed. (We had in actuality already built the refrigerator box in David's basement and taken it to the cabin, in case anyone later checked out our story.)

Finally, the great day came. After school, David picked up Bill and me, and we gathered our groceries and sleeping bags and checked to see that we had everything we needed. We had nine sleeping bags and three big bags of groceries. Our plan for the evening's dinner was to cook spaghetti and have it with rolls. We had cooking pots for the wood stove and all the food supplies we needed to make a good impression with our cooking. We also had a large tarp in the back of the truck. We arranged it over the food and the sleeping bags. The truck was a 1954 Chevrolet Model 4100, not a big monster truck like those that appeared on the scene years later. It had a plain bench seat that would at best hold only the three of us boys, so the girls would have to ride in the back. Besides, this was the only way we could be sure that they were well hidden and completely out of sight under the tarp.

So we were off. The names of those six dear girls will not be documented here, as all but one of them are very much alive. Even in our own memories, we prefer to hold them merely as "the camping-trip girls." One at a time, they were picked up and secured under the tarp in the back. We could hear them giggling and talking from where we were in the front, and we had to keep telling Bill, who was seated next to the passenger-side door, to lean out the window and tell them to stay quiet.

Once we were all loaded, we started out for Ratcliffe Cove

Road, the access to Big Stomp Mountain. The dirt road up the mountain turned off the pavement just beyond my aunt Esther's house and right beside the Ratcliffe Cove Baptist Church. It was also almost straight across the road from Mr. West's house. We had to have Bill jump out quickly and open the gate, then close it behind the Chevy and hop back in the front, so that we did not attract any visitors wanting to make conversation on our way. It was just starting to rain as Bill got back into the truck.

It was not more than a couple of miles up the mountain to the cabin, but the old road was very washed out and rocky, and the driver, now David, had to go slowly and carefully and be sure that the wheels stayed on the highest parts of the road along the way. As we crept along, the rain got harder and harder. Soon, we had all the windows rolled up and the wipers running full speed.

It was raining so very hard by now that we could not hear the girls screaming in the back of the truck. We had not secured the tarp over the edges of the truck bed because that would have involved too much planning and work. And that also would have made it too hard to get the girls each quickly under cover as we picked them up. No, instead, we had just tucked it in loosely around them, the food, and the sleeping bags. This meant that instead of keeping the rain off them, it collected it very efficiently and kept all of the water inside the truck bed. We did not know that all the contents—girls, food, sleeping bags—were now sitting in about six inches of rainwater. They were screaming needlessly.

Soon, the road itself looked like we were driving up a creek bed, as the heavy water came pouring down the roadway more easily that it could run through the woods.

Just up ahead of us, now about halfway to the cabin, there was a creek that the road crossed. There was never a bridge of any kind, just a little ford through the normally small stream. On this day, however, there was nothing small about it. The little creek was filled flush with its banks, and we had no choice but to try to drive through it in the Chevy truck.

David shifted the truck into low gear, then hit the water with a good bit of force. The water came over the hood in a wave just as the rear end of the truck floated sideways in the rushing creek. Suddenly, we were turned perpendicular to the road and sitting, totally stuck, off the road in the creek bed. There was to be no movement at all until all this water was gone. We were stuck.

Bill looked over to the right of the road. "Look!" He was cheerful. "There's an old barn right over there. We can get everything out of the back and stay in that barn and maybe get the truck out in the morning." This summarized the only plan that there was in our present world.

When we got out of the truck and waded around to the back, the tarp was totally motionless. It looked like the girls had dug themselves into deep hibernation under the cover. There was just a series of motionless lumps filling the bed of the truck. Then we lifted the tarp.

As soon as they saw us, they began to wail. Vocabulary lessons followed. There was blaming sufficient to last for several years and the invention of various new names with which we were destined to be stuck for some time to come.

We tried to assure them that it was not as bad as they thought and that we were totally competent to take very good care of them in any circumstance of nature. They did not even reply to this little speech. They just looked at us with total disgust.

"Come on." Bill was the most reassuring one of us. "See that nice barn over there? That will be even a better place on a night like this than the cabin. All of you run right over there and get in the dry barn, and we will bring all of the food and other supplies."

There was nothing left for the six sopping girls to do but head for the barn.

Once they were out of the truck, the three of us boys tried to assemble what was left there for us to carry. The paper bags of food were totally disintegrated by the soaking water. We simply gathered up the groceries and made several trips to carry them to safety. The sleeping bags were something else altogether. The first one I picked up felt like it weighed forty pounds and had water literally pouring out of it as I tried to carry it to the barn. I am not sure why we even bothered to carry all of those sleeping bags from the truck, as it would be a very long time before anyone would want to crawl into them.

So now we were in the driest place possible in our present circumstances. The old barn did have some leaks, but it was much better than being out in the open. Also, it had a lot of old hay bales, and we actually created what looked like a small room surrounded with hay bales to block the wind and give us some sense of security. We scattered several bales of hay on the floor of the barn where we could have places to sit that were dry and seemed to be somewhat warm.

"So," I said, "I think I'll get our supper started. See, girls, we really did come prepared for anything. Right here, we have a little Primus stove for cooking our supper. We do not even need a wood stove or a fireplace. I'm going to cook outside the 'hay room,' so there won't be a chance of setting the hay on fire. We don't need a fire after all this rain."

I gathered up the spaghetti (it was already getting soft from being soaked in rainwater in the truck bed), the sauce, a can of mushrooms, two aluminum pots, and the Primus stove. One of the girls volunteered to help me with the food. We went outside the hay-bale enclosure, and I set up the stove near the edge of the floor by the barn door.

We had no water for cooking, but we were right beside the creek. Maybe the creek water looked muddy, but it was only going to be used for cooking the spaghetti and then would be drained off. Besides, the boiling of the water in cooking would kill any germs that happened to be in it. I took the larger pot down to the creek and carefully filled it with water as clear as I could get.

Then the cooking started. The stove was fired up and the big pot balanced on top of the small burner to work toward boiling. I added salt and butter to the water, waiting for it to boil. When it came to a boil, I slowly worked the two packages of spaghetti into the water. Then the spaghetti was boiling happily. Between times of giving it a stir so it would not glob together, I opened the two cans of spaghetti sauce and the can of mushrooms.

Since the little stove had just one burner, it seemed like it was not really convenient to heat up the sauce in a second pot. My idea was to let the spaghetti boil until it was tender, then carefully drain off the water in which it had cooked. After that, I would add more butter, pour the sauce into the big pot with the noodles, add the mushrooms, and stir the whole meal carefully until everything was well mixed and uniformly hot. It was a good plan.

In a few more minutes, the spaghetti was cooked just enough.

"How about telling everyone that we are almost ready to eat? They can all get a paper plate and some plastic utensils we brought and come out here, where we can serve ourselves. Then we can go back into the hay room and eat where it is warmer."

Everyone gathered up and came out to where I was cooking just as I was pouring the sauce into the big pot of cooked spaghetti noodles.

All went well as the two cans of sauce covered the noodles. All went well as more butter was added. All went well as the can of mushrooms was poured onto the mixture. All seemed to be going well as I took a big spoon and began to stir the entire concoction to make it well blended and evenly bubbling hot. Then something happened.

The pot was far too large and much too heavy to stay happily balanced on the tiny Primus burner. As I gave it a big stir, the pot tumbled off of the burner, fell down from the barn floor, and hit the ground. The entire glob of spaghetti and sauce plopped out of the big pot and began to roll, all clinging together like a huge mass of worms, down through the grove of hemlock trees. The rolling ball began to pick up a covering of brown, fallen hemlock needles until it soon took on the appearance of a fleeing baby porcupine. Not only the six girls but all nine of us stood there silently watching our entire hot supper disappear from us into the darkness.

No one said anything because there was simply nothing to be said. There was a long time of silence before we decided to see whether there was any food at all that was redeemable after being soaked in the back of the truck. All the bread was ruined, as were the crackers and cookies and everything else that had been boxed from the store. The only things we could find that were not ruined were cans and jars. These, however, had the labels soaked off of them from the water, and it was impossible to tell what might be in each one.

We were so starved by now that we had to make a guess at it. We ended up having a meal of canned dried beef, accompanied by canned sliced peaches. It was actually not as bad as it sounds.

After the "meal," we tried to figure out how we were going to manage to sleep. The soaked sleeping bags were out of the question. We were very lucky in that there was a lot of baled hay in the old barn. We ended up making what could only be described as large personal nests out of hay and gradually settling down to try to find a compromise between sleeping and freezing for the night. No one in the entire group was happy about anything, and we knew that the girls were even less happy than were the three of us boys.

Gradually, the rain stopped, and the sound of water dripping from the trees filled our night. Time passed with infinite slowness. I kept falling asleep, then quickly waking up to check my watch and discover that only about fifteen minutes had passed since the last time I had checked it.

Way in the night, I began to hear a strange sound. It was not loud or heavy, just a regularly repeated *thunk, thunk, thunk*, like someone regularly striking a rock over and over again with some sort of wooden stick. The sound got closer and closer, and then Bill and I (we were both awake) could see a light coming up the road we had traveled through the woods. We quickly roused the others so we would have help in case it was the arrival of danger.

The moving light seemed to find the swamped Chevy pickup and shine all around it. Then it crossed the little creek, now settled back to normal, and the thunking sound resumed. As it came closer, we could see that it was a man dressed in a long raincoat and hat. He was walking with a walking stick and carrying a flashlight. Then we could see: it was my daddy!

To this very day, I have not been able to put together all of the pieces of separate information he had to discover and then string together in the proper sequence in order to show up when and where he did on that night. I knew I was dead!

Daddy looked at all of us, and we all looked at him. No one tried to hide; there was no point in that. We simply all stared at each other.

Then he said, "Looks like all of you might need a ride out of here. Follow me."

We left everything, including the truck, behind for the time being. Then we all fell into line, following his yellow flashlight beam down the road off the mountain. He didn't talk at all, just led the way.

When we got to the bottom where the dirt road joined the paved road, three cars were parked right there in the Baptist church parking lot. One was Daddy's Plymouth. I did not recognize the other two. As it turned out, they were being driven by two of the young women whom I knew to be tellers who worked with Daddy at the bank in town. Daddy assigned three of the girls to each of these two cars, and the three of us boys got into the backseat of his car. No one wanted to ride in the front, where any kind of conversation might be expected.

(We later learned that the six girls were not taken home that night. No, instead of a ride home, they were taken quietly to Ruth Alexander's house. Ruth Alexander was our high-school biology teacher. She was also our youth-group counselor at church. We were eventually told that after an undescribed night at her house, they were each silently and singly spirited home the next day, so that none of their parents ever had any idea at all what had happened on that night.)

Daddy silently started the Plymouth and began to drive toward our house. It was not unusual for David and Bill to stay over at our house, and on this night I thought they might be protection from my being killed immediately. It must have worked. When we got home, my mother did not appear, though I am certain she was not asleep.

Daddy offered, "Do you boys need anything to eat before you go to bed?"

David answered him. "No, sir. We had a good supper earlier, and we're all ready now for some sleep."

Daddy went to his and Mama's bedroom. The three of us went to my bedroom. The night passed, and I have no memory of ever falling to sleep.

Uncle Grover was right. The true nature of punishment is mental. We would all have been happy if Daddy had lined us up in the garage and beat us with sticks. But he did not. He did not even say a word or acknowledge the events of the night. He just went to bed and left us to worry.

In the night, Bill said, "Does your daddy have a gun in the house?"

"He has two of them: a .22 and a shotgun," I answered.

No one said anything more about that. We were worried and scared to death. The night passed with profound slowness.

"What do you think he knows?" David asked.

"I am scared even to think about it," was my only answer.

"I am scared of what's going to happen in the morning," Bill added.

We all figured that the breakfast table would be the courtroom.

The next morning, we all showered and got ourselves looking as nice as possible before appearing in the kitchen. When we arrived, Mama was making pancakes and Daddy was reading the paper and drinking a cup of coffee. We sat down. He did not say a word. I thought maybe he was waiting until David and Bill were gone before he confronted me, so I played along and entered into the normal breakfast conversation with the others.

After breakfast, I had to take the boys home. As soon as they were delivered, I was scared to go home. I drove around town for a little while, trying to put off what I was certain would be the end of me. Finally, I gave up and went home.

It was Saturday, and by now Daddy was watching a football game on television while Mama was sitting in the same room making out her grocery list. I sat down and tried to act interested in the ball game while waiting for the inevitable. It never came. Daddy started commenting on the football game and initiating normal conversation while time dragged on. Soon, I decided that he was now waiting for Mama to go to the grocery store so he could have me all to himself. That way, I could be killed and he could clean up all the mess before she got home. It was a miserable game of waiting.

Finally, Mama finished her list. "I'm going to go to the store," she said to Daddy. "Is there anything that either one of you wants me to get for you?"

I almost chuckled. Why should I need anything when my life was about to come to an end? I told her that there was not a thing I could think of that I needed. Daddy cheerfully told her the same thing. She went out the door.

As soon as she was gone, Daddy got up from his chair and went into the kitchen. He came back in a few minutes with a fresh cup of coffee, sat down in his chair, and focused on the television. Nothing was said. I was sweating by now and almost ready to confess to anything just to get it over with. The ball game rolled on. Nothing was said.

By the time that day came to an end, I was a nervous wreck. I couldn't imagine what he was planning, but it had to be bad. That night, I couldn't sleep and was really getting exhausted from lack of rest and proper eating. It was pure misery.

The next day was Sunday. I did not offer any of my usual excuses about getting out of going to church. No, I wanted him to see that I was indeed anxious to go to both Sunday school and church so I could atone for my sins. Daddy acted like it was a normal day. He sang to himself as he got ready, just like he did each Sunday as he thought through and picked out the songs he would suggest as the Sunday-school song leader. We had our normal Sunday breakfast of pancakes with bacon. By now, I was so starved that I managed to eat some.

All that day, nothing was said about the camping trip. The same pattern continued through the coming week. Each day as I waited for him to come home from work, I expected a conviction to come. It never came. Two weeks passed. Nothing was said.

Sometime during that time, we were out for a family Sunday-afternoon ride and Daddy happened to turn the car out through Ratcliffe Cove. "We haven't gone out to see Uncle Mark and Aunt Esther for a while. Maybe this would be a good time to stop off there."

When we got to their house, Daddy did not drive into their driveway. "I think I'll just pull over here into the church parking lot in case Mark needs to get his car out of the driveway."

He drove right in and parked exactly where his car and the other two cars had been parked when they came to pick us all up during the night of the camping trip. When he got out of the car, he looked up the dirt road toward Big Stomp Mountain like he was expecting someone he knew to come down the road. Nothing was said.

We all walked across the yard to visit Mark and Esther. I was in a full sweat. We were back very close to the scene of the crime. Daddy did not even look at me.

Once we were in the house, Aunt Esther and Uncle Mark were cheerful and glad to see us. We sat in the kitchen and talked. I thought we would never leave. They talked about everything on the face of the earth, but no mention was made of my habitual camping near their house. It was a miserable afternoon. Finally, we went home. Nothing was said.

Nothing was ever said.

It has now been fifty-five years since the camping-with-the-girls night. Daddy has been dead since 1993. Any reasonable person would think all of those memories would be safely forgotten and over by now. But I know better.

Each night, while most of the population of the world falls peacefully asleep, I still roll around in my bed in search of sleep because, who knows? Tonight might be the very night when he chooses to come back and confront me.

The Grand Canyon

During all of my growing-up years, Daddy worked at the bank. Because he worked with money all the time, Daddy tried to teach me all that he could about money.

He taught me that, in those 1950s days when people threw their trash out the car window, I could go along the roadsides and search out those old, green, thick-glass Coca-Cola bottles that had been tossed there. There was a two-cent deposit on those bottles, and if I collected them, I could take them up to Turk Owen's store and Tommy Owen would give me the cash for them.

He taught me to go through the closets carefully and search out the coat hangers that were not bent and had no rust on them. Some of these had my mama's clothes on them, but the clothes could be moved. If I could collect one hundred good coat hangers and take them up to Harrell's Cleaners, LeRoy Harrell would give a dollar for them.

I even learned from him how to get my schoolteachers to hire me to mow their lawns and rake their leaves. "All you have to do," Daddy prompted me, "is to threaten to fail and be back in their rooms again next year, and they will hire you on the spot."

I loved all these little ways I could make small amounts of cash that I could take to the store and spend without having to give any accounting to my parents.

Daddy, however, had one strong warning for me: "Remember, son, no matter how much money you make in all these ways, these are not real jobs."

"Why aren't they jobs?" I needed to know.

"Because you get money for doing them."

"Isn't that the whole idea?" I asked.

He was quick to respond. "No! It's not a real job until you have to work for a week or two without any money being exchanged, then you have to wait for a check."

I was terribly disappointed. I would rather just have money and be able to spend all of it on the way home from wherever I had earned it.

Finally, I graduated from high school and got my first "real" job. I was working at the Cokesbury Book Store at the Methodist assembly grounds, called Lake Junaluska, only about a mile and a half from where we lived. Each day, I would eagerly go to work, where I was falling in love with books and earning minimum wage. The first week, I would ease over to the side of the store every couple of hours so I could figure out how much I had made so far; it was already spent in my imagination. So, when the end of the first week came, I knew exactly to the penny how much my check was going to be—until it came.

I opened the envelope with my check in it, and when I looked at the check, about a third of what I was supposed to get was gone! That's when I first learned about taxes!

"I don't like having a real job," I complained to Daddy. "They steal your money!"

He laughed. "They didn't steal your money. Look at the little stub on the check. They just took out your taxes. They have to do that with everybody."

"Why do they take out taxes from me? This is just my first job."

"Doesn't matter," he responded. "They need your taxes just like they need mine. They need to build schools, they need to pave roads—all kinds of things." I think he chose these two things thinking that they would make an impression on me. It did not work.

"I just finished school," I insisted. "And you hardly ever let me drive a car. I really don't care if the roads get paved."

My father did not want me to be discouraged by my first experience with taxation. A couple of days later, he came home carrying a large package under his arm. "I brought you something to read," he said as he dropped the heavy package on the kitchen table.

To this day, I do not know where he had obtained a printed and bound copy of the United States federal budget.

"I want you to read this," he started. "There will be things in there that you like. Here is what you do. Read this big budget until you come to something that you really like. Then look down at the bottom of the section and see how much is going to be spent on that one item in one year. If you think about it, you will realize that you will never pay that much in taxes in your entire life. So here is what you do next. Tear that page out and keep it in a safe place after you have decided that that budget item belongs just to you. That way, each time you pay taxes, you will be paying only for what you have chosen as your own private interest. That will make you feel a whole lot better."

At that moment, I thought this was the most ridiculous idea I had ever heard of in my life. I was very surprised when what he suggested actually worked!

Where we lived in Waynesville, we could look out our kitchen window and see the growing scar wrapping around the mountains as the last miles of the Blue Ridge Parkway were being built toward its southern end in Cherokee, North Carolina. In addition to that, we could get in our family car and in less than thirty minutes, driving in any of three different directions, we could be inside the Great Smoky Mountains National Park. So, when I came to the section covering the National Park Service, I decided that all of the tax money I paid for my entire life would go to make payments on national parks.

I have now been doing that for more than fifty years. So, thanks to my daddy's direction, I now consider that I am the personal owner of our national parks!

My wife, Merle, and I live on Ocracoke Island off the coast of North Carolina. Ocracoke Island is approximately twenty-eight hundred acres, twenty-one hundred of which are part of Cape Hatteras National Seashore, a national park property. Many people not familiar with our island do not know of this park connection. They hear that we live on an island, and they often say, "Wow, do you own the island?"

I smile and calmly say, "Yes, almost all of it. But we are not selfish, so we are happy for you to come there and visit our sixteen-mile beach."

We travel each year, often more than 250 days, to storytelling events and engagements all over the country. Sometimes, people learn about that and their question is, "How do you stay away from home so much?"

"Well," I want to answer, "we don't actually stay away from home at all. We own other places. Since we added the state of Delaware, we now own property in every single state and even territories of the United States."

Each year, we travel to the Timpanogos Storytelling Festival in Utah. We love to visit the state of Utah. We own most of the bottom third of the whole state. And once in a while, we get to go up to work in Alaska for a couple of weeks. Two weeks in Alaska are hardly enough time to even write down the names of all of our properties there.

In the summer of 1991, Merle and I were traveling west, going from one storytelling event to another, mainly on the Interstate 40 route. On our first night from home, we stopped in Waynesville to visit my parents. As we talked with my daddy about the upcoming trip, I reminded him of what he had taught me about taxes. I told him about my "properties" and let him know that on the upcom-

Standing with Mama and Joe at the old Clingmans Dome
lookout tower around 1954

ing trip we were planning to visit as many of our properties as
possible.

He laughed and then said, "You know, that was a good idea
you had back then. Now, if you ever need the money, you can sell
them off one at a time. I bet they have appreciated a lot in value
since 1962."

The next day, we said goodbye and started the trip by driving
across Newfound Gap and through the Great Smoky Mountains
National Park, the one that had given me the purchase idea to

begin with. After taking a small detour to spend the night at Hot Springs National Park in Arkansas, we got back on the I-40 route and proceeded west, visiting the Petrified Forest and Mesa Verde on our way.

While we were on that part of our trip, we had planned a big visit at one of our major properties we had never visited before. We called it "the Grand Canyon." Turning off I-40 at Williams, Arizona, we headed north. The first sign that we were on the right highway said, "Grand Canyon, 68 miles." We were getting excited now. As the road rolled on, the signs periodically reminded us of the distance—forty miles, thirty-five miles, ten miles.

When the ten-mile sign appeared, I knew that something was wrong. After all, growing up in the Smoky Mountains, I was accustomed to parkland that stuck up in the air so you could see it coming. We got all the way down to three miles and I still could see nothing up there. *We are too late!* I thought. *There is absolutely nothing here. We have missed it.*

Then the road ended and we came to a parking lot marked "Mather Point"—obviously named for Stephen Mather, the first director of the National Park Service. We pulled into a parking space, and I said to Merle, "We've never been here before, so I have an idea."

"What is it this time?" she replied, with the advantage of experience.

"Let's not look."

"What are you talking about?"

"I mean, let's not just stroll out there and casually look like it's simply one more piece of scenery. Let me come around there and get you, then let's close our eyes and hold hands and ease up to the edge. Then, when we are both ready, we can open our eyes and see what we've paid for!"

She reluctantly agreed. We got together, eyes closed and hands held, and eased toward the rim of the canyon. It was a very good thing that the park had put a railing around that part.

When we got there and opened our eyes, all we could do was stop breathing, start crying, and back up! It was beautiful!

No matter how many photographs we had seen of the Grand Canyon, nothing ever began to capture the total peripheral scope of our own eyes. And it did not stand still. All afternoon, it changed as the cloud shadows moved across the land and the sun changed the colors and cliff tones within the canyon itself. We could not walk away from it.

We were looking deep into the depths of the canyon when we saw something moving. It was near a glimpse of the Colorado River but was so far down that we could not tell what it was until I went back to the car and got the binoculars. Then, when we looked, we could clearly see that it was a little string of mules with people riding on them.

When we were planning our trip, I had discovered that you could take mule rides at the Grand Canyon. There were a couple of choices: You could ride a mule partway down and then back up again in the same day, or you could go for the whole shebang. You could ride a mule all the way down to Phantom Ranch, spend the night there, and then ride back out on the day after that.

My wife, Merle, has always loved to ride. She grew up with horses and had a horse when she was a child. She loves horses, and I love her. So we were, in fact, signed up to start out the next morning, ride mules to the bottom, spend the night there, and come back out on the following day. It was going to be great. We were going to get to go into the depths of the Grand Canyon, and we ourselves would not even have to do the walking or carrying.

Finally, the sun went down, and we went down into the village and checked into our hotel. Our confirmation letter told us that at a certain time after dinner that evening we were to report to "the mule center" at Bright Angel Lodge to turn ourselves in and get our "final" instructions.

As soon as we were checked in at the mule center, the first thing that they did was to weigh us. Just imagine meeting a group of twelve complete strangers—you do not know their names, you do not know where they come from, you do not know what they do for a living, but you already know who weighs more than you and who weighs less than you. They tried to tell us that they had to check to see that we were not too heavy and would mash a mule flat. I could not help thinking, *What kind of way is that to start off?*

I did not yet know that the Fred Harvey Company, which has always run the mule trips, has a huge supply of mules, most of which come from the Reese Brothers Mule Farm in Gallatin, Tennessee. Those Reese Brothers mules weigh up to twelve hundred pounds. King Kong could have ridden on one of their mules, and the mule wouldn't have even felt him.

We gradually figured that the weighing business was just the first step in an escalating intimidation process.

After we were all weighed in, we were given clipboards like you get when you go to a new doctor's office. On the clipboards were pages with questions. We were instructed to check the right answers and then sign our name at the bottom and add the date.

The first question was, "Are you sure you want to ride a mule into the Grand Canyon?" Answer: "Yes."

Second question: "Do you understand that you could be seriously injured or killed riding a mule into the Grand Canyon?" Answer: "Yes."

Next question: "Do you care if you are seriously injured or killed riding a mule into the Grand Canyon?" Right answer: "No!"

Next question: "Do you care if after tomorrow your family never sees you again?" Right answer: "No."

Last question: "Are you happy to pay three hundred dollars in advance just to get to die this way?" Final answer: "Yes!"

After we signed at the bottom of the page, we went back up to our room and tried to sleep, thinking about all of that. Then, early the next morning, six o'clock, we were up and at the mule corral to meet our own personal mules and our guide, a lovely and much-experienced woman named Shirley.

The first thing that Shirley did was to line us all up in weight order. Then she explained how it worked. The heaviest person won the biggest mule and then, right on down the line it went, until the lightest person got the smallest mule. I ended up somewhere in the middle, but I did notice that everyone was looking to see who won the biggest mule. It was a woman from Texas who told us her name was Mary but that, like her friends back at home, we should call her "Fluffy."

Once the mules were assigned, there was instruction to follow. "Look at those mules," Shirley started. (Where else did she think we were looking?) "Those mules are not going down in the Grand Canyon today because they want to go. They have already been. The only reason they are going back down there is because you want to go, and you have to help them."

She then handed out little switches that looked like they were made of twisted-up coat hanger wires and told us that while we were riding along, we had to smack our mules constantly on the flank to keep their noses right up under the tail of the mule in front of us.

"What's that all about?" someone asked.

"That's about safety," Shirley was quick to reply. "You see, these mules have been down in there so many times that as they walk along, they fall asleep. When they are sleepwalking, they tend to fall behind the mule in front of them. Then they stumble and wake up, and when they wake up and see that they have fallen behind, they run to catch up. They do not care where or how they run. These mules are smart. They know that if you fall off, they get the next two days off!"

Not my mule, I thought. *We are going to stay right up there in line where we are supposed to be.*

"Another thing," she went on. "You may notice that these mules like to walk right on the edge of the trail. We think they like to look down in there. You don't want to look down in there? The mules don't care! Don't lean away from the edge. That just throws them off balance, and they get even closer to the edge to make up for it."

Not me, I thought again. *I am going to sit straight up in the saddle for the entire adventure.*

Shirley's speech was winding down now. "Now, if any of you

have decided that you do not want to make this trip, we always have a waiting list. So, if you want to get your money back and not go, that is possible right now. But if you decide to go and get on your mule, there is no turning back."

One large man, the only one of us who could actually talk at the time, got his money back. The rest of us, including that man's own wife and two children, didn't know any better, and we were on our way.

We started out down the Bright Angel Trail. The Bright Angel Trail is wide and open and beautiful. Right near the start, we passed through a charming little tunnel arch. In a short time, the trail was zigzagging back and forth down the side of the canyon wall, and we dropped deeper and deeper into its depth. I was looking down at the trail as it came back right under us, and I thought, *What is the big deal? I can look right down there and see the trail I am heading for. Why, I could jump off my mule and still land on the trail. This is going to be easy. They were just overdoing the warnings to keep us on our toes. Nothing to it!*

We went down about four and a half miles and stopped at a place called Indian Gardens for a picnic lunch. There was a water source at Indian Gardens, and after we ate, Shirley suggested that we might want to wet our clothes to help keep us cool, as from here on it might get uncomfortably hot for a while. Most everyone doused water over their clothes and hats and carefully refilled the bota bags we carried for drinking water.

Now, we began to ride toward the inner part of the canyon, where it drops down to the Colorado River. We were riding across the Tonto Plateau, and at that time I did not know a single word of Spanish. I did not understand that in that language, native to the Grand Canyon before English arrived, the word *tonto* hits the ground about halfway between *foolish* and flat *stupid*.

We got out toward the edge of the plateau, and Shirley said, "Well, folks, we're about to come to the River Trail."

Someone asked, "You mean we're already down to the river?"

"Oh, no," came her reply. "It's just that from this next curve on we can always see the river."

"How far down is it to the river?" asked the same questioner.

"By the trail or straight down?" Shirley wanted to be clear.

"Straight down, as we look at it."

"Oh, that." She didn't even smile. "I'd say about six or seven hundred feet."

You can go to church on Sunday, pick up the Bible, and read all the creation stories in the book of Genesis, and you will find no mention of the day on which the River Trail was made. No, if you notice carefully, each account of a creation day ends with these words: "It was good."

No, the creator did not think we needed a River Trail. The creator was happy with a crack in the rock running about seven hundred feet above the Colorado River. It was Franklin Delano Roosevelt, the Civilian Conservation Corps, and five hundred thousand pounds of dynamite that sent young Depression-era farm boys from Iowa, Texas, and Oklahoma to blast that little crack into a shelf about four feet wide. And when they finished, since they were never going back there again, they called it a trail.

Those big twelve-hundred-pound mules from Gallatin, Tennessee, seem like they are about four feet wide, but they don't use the whole trail. No, they walk right over on the edge. And they are so big around that when you look down you cannot see the ground. After you look down your own leg and it runs out thirty-something inches later, you keep looking straight down seven hundred feet to the Colorado River.

Suddenly, I remembered what it did to my stomach when I used to watch movies on old black-and-white television in which someone climbed out on the ledge of a tall building and threatened to jump. I could look down and see the tiny cars and people down below. Those twenty-story buildings were only about a third as tall as the distance between us and the Colorado River. And we couldn't step back because we were stuck on top of mules that liked to be right on the edge.

You could look past their necks and see their feet working, but I shall tell you quickly, that didn't work. These mules had it all worked out so that they could take a step and make it look like they were going to miss the trail. Then, at the last possible moment, they would put their hoof back on the trail. After you watched that for a few moments, you did not need to see it anymore. In about fifteen minutes, I decided that I had seen my entire three hundred dollars' worth. But there was no way back!

I thought about things as well as I could for a person who had stopped breathing, and gradually figured out what I was going to do. I got a good grip on the mule's sides with my knees, I got a fresh hold on the saddle horn with both hands, I turned my head sideways to the right while I closed my left eye, and for the next four hours I did up-close one-eyed geological studies of the rock formations of the wall of the Grand Canyon. I had no idea what was on my left side. We could have gone right through Walmart and I would never have known the difference.

Throughout that entire trip, I had a thirty-five-millimeter camera hanging around my neck. I do not have one single picture of the mule trip.

Every once in a while, Shirley would call us to a halt for a few moments. The first time, she gave us careful instructions: "When we stop on this trail, be sure that your mule is facing out over the edge when we stop."

When I asked why, the answer was clear: "That's because if a wild animal or a falling rock happens to startle them, their instinct is to jump backwards."

Okay, I got it. We stopped, and I obeyed. I pulled my mule (her name was "Su-leen") at an angle until her head was over the rim of the trail. About that time, she spotted a little sprig of green grass that was growing about a foot below the lip of the trail and decided she had to have that small bite of grass. As she stretched down to get it, her back looked to me just like a steeply angled sliding board that was aimed toward landing me in the Colorado River. That's when both eyes closed!

After what felt like innumerable hours, it suddenly grew dark. I looked up to see what was happening and discovered that the trail had entered a short tunnel that was carved through the canyon rock. At the other end of the tunnel, cables growing out of the rock were supporting a wire swinging bridge that was to carry the trail sixty feet above the Colorado River for what looked like a hundred miles to the other side.

When Su-leen and I got up to the swinging bridge, it seemed that every place I looked at it, I could see straight through it. I thought to myself, *Which eye am I going to close this time?* I decided that, for a mere three hundred dollars, that mule had had all the help from me she was going to get. So it was another time to close both eyes! I got a good, fresh grip on the saddle horn, held my breath, and counted every time the mule's left front hoof hit the bridge. We had to come back this same way in the morning, and I figured I could then just count backward and live through getting back across. I can tell you with some authority that it is 151 mule steps across the Colorado River.

We made it to the other side. The trail curved down and around under the end of the bridge and up Bright Angel Creek to Phantom Ranch. Once we were off the mules and safely in the bottom of the canyon, the rest of the day was great. We had a big cookout steak dinner and all tried to talk like we had had a good day. We were actually down there on the Fourth of July, and the temperature was 118 degrees. After the meal was finished, everyone got a big cup of fresh ice. We went outside and piled the ice in a little pile like it was a campfire and sat around it trying to cool off.

After a little while, Shirley came out and sat down to join us. She proceeded to tell us stories about other mule trips. She told us about one trip on which a man fell off of his mule. They were not even out of the corral yet when, as he was getting up on the mule, he slipped back and fell to the ground with his left foot stuck in the stirrup. Not knowing what was happening, the mule started to run and was dragging the man with it. Everything would have been fine, but as they passed a little cedar tree, the fallen man reached out and grabbed hold of it. The mule did not even slow down, and it pulled the man's leg off!

"It's okay, it's okay!" he kept yelling as everyone ran over to where he was lying on the ground. "I've got another one back up in the room." That's when they discovered that he had a prosthetic leg.

"For about ten seconds, I was sure we had killed him!" was Shirley's laughing conclusion to the little story.

She told us about the early days, before the swinging bridge was built, when a single steel cable crossed the Colorado River. A wheel ran on this cable holding a big metal basket underneath on its trip across the river. She told us to look at the pictures back inside Phantom Ranch and we would see that a mule could actually be fit into the metal basket and sent across the river. We did not ask how people got across. None of us wanted to know anything about that.

After a while, Shirley said, "Well, folks, it's getting pretty late, and we have an early start in the morning. So I think we all better get up and go to bed."

Going to bed sounded great, but after that day on the mules not a single one of us could get up. Shirley had to come around behind where we were all sitting on the circle of logs and lever us into an upright position. Merle and I had four legs between the two of us, and not a one of them was worth anything. We could sort of scoot up to the cabin where we were staying for the night. We could reach up and turn the knob and get the door open, but we could not get inside the cabin itself. There were two steps, and we had no way to conquer them. Finally, we figured that all we could do was turn around, sit down on the bottom step, and use our hands and arms to push us backward up into the cabin.

We had planned this trip so far ahead of time that we were actually the first people to sign up for this day. And that, we were proudly told, was the reason that, instead of bunk beds, we had been given the one and only double bed at Phantom Ranch.

Big deal! We got in that bed side by side, and our legs, all on their own, insisted on spreading out until we had pushed one another right out of the bed on either side. The only way we could figure out how to sleep in the same bed was to put one head up in the left corner at the top and the other head over in the opposite corner at the bottom, so our legs could have their own way without hurting one another.

And then, after very little sleep, we were up in the morning and back on the mules. It worked this way because, unless you were fortunate enough to die in the night, this was the only way you could get back out of there.

We started off on this day's journey and made it back across the swinging bridge without incident. We were, however, not going back today on the River Trail. No, once on the other side of the river, after a few turns, we turned off up a trail called the South Kaibab Trail, which Shirley told us was too steep to ride down. But if we would hold on, we could go up that way.

This will be better, I thought. *We will be going uphill all day. I can just look down at the ground and get out of here.*

It didn't work that way. As we started up the South Kaibab Trail, the route would go out toward a point above the river where it would begin to drop off on both sides. The trail would get more and more narrow before it made an abrupt switchback. At the switchback, the mules didn't even pretend to watch where they were going. It looked for all the world like they just kept going until they had taken about two steps out into thin air. Then they swung around and were somehow miraculously back on the trail again.

On top of this, when we got to the highest possible point above the river, Fluffy stopped her mule. Then she proclaimed in a loud voice, "Oh, look how beautiful it is! Look how far down it is!"

All I could think was, *Shut up!*

After a mile or two of this, I could not take it anymore. I raised my hand in the air and called out, "Shirley! I need to walk a little bit."

"What for?" was her immediate question.

"I just need to, that's all," was my also-quick answer.

She thought I needed to go to the bathroom and for some

reason would not say that. She didn't need to worry about that. I couldn't go to the bathroom for three weeks after this trip.

She presented her case. "You can't walk. Over the long haul, people cannot walk as fast as the mules, and we would lose you. We have to stay together, and the only way to do that is for everyone to stay on their mule." She suggested that we take a fifteen-minute break and that I get off the mule for a few minutes and breathe deeply.

I responded to that suggestion: "I don't want to take a break. Every time we take a break, it takes longer to get out of here. I have another idea. Let me walk ahead a little bit. That way, I can't get lost or separated from everyone else. Just let me walk ahead while everyone else takes a break."

Finally, Shirley agreed. "Okay. You can start out ahead of us, but after this break, when we catch up with you, you must get back on your mule. That's all there is to it."

I agreed.

So I started up the South Kaibab Trail alone, ahead of the mules. Once I rounded a turn in the trail, those mules never saw me again. There was not a mule west of the Mississippi River that could have caught me if I had to get on its back. Over the remaining five miles, I beat the mules to the top by forty-five minutes.

Once back at the top, I thought all the trouble was over. But I had not counted on what this trip was still to do to me at night. I would fall asleep, and then a dream would start. I would begin to dream that I was riding a mule directly toward the rim of the Grand Canyon. As we got close to the rim, I could see that there was a tight wire stretched from the near rim of the canyon all the way to the far-side rim. Once at the edge, my mule would step out and begin to walk the tight wire toward the far rim. As we got out into the air, I would suddenly wake up in a terrible sweat. Then I would get calmed down and fall back to sleep, only to have the same dream start back up over and over again. It was exhausting.

After a few nights of this sleep deprivation, I decided to call my daddy. I told him all about the trip and about what was happening now. I had no idea or intention that he might have a curative suggestion. I just wanted to share the pain with him.

Then he reminded me, "You know, you own all of that property."

"What?" I had forgotten for a moment.

"Of course," he went on, "it's one of your own personal national parks. And since it is yours, you could just sell it if you want to. That might take care of it!"

I suddenly thought that he might have hit on something, and began that night's sleep with a plan to dispose of one of my pieces of property.

It worked! As soon as I knew I was in control of my property, the dreams ceased, and I did not have to sell after all.

So my daddy saved the Grand Canyon from being sold to some water company or power company that would no doubt have built dams and run wires and drilled holes until, in no time, even the River Trail would have disappeared. And I am still paying taxes so that, forever, people can go see the Grand Canyon.

The Drunk Chicken

When Daddy's father, my grandfather, was in the North Carolina legislature, he introduced a bill that in 1909 brought prohibition to North Carolina a full decade before the Volstead Act made it national law. Whether this was done because of his Methodist teetotaling conscience or to protect the business of his bootlegging mountain neighbors, no one knows. Whatever his reason, I grew up in a household in which even the fumes of alcohol never came through the door.

Since, when you are growing up, your friends are likely to be the children of your parents' friends, there was no real acquaintance with spirituous liquor among my entire circle of teenage associates. This meant that, when we all went off to college, we had a lot to learn. To be very clear, the drinking age in North Carolina was eighteen years old at the time, so there was nothing that legally prevented any of us from buying or consuming alcohol. It was just that none of us had any experiential knowledge of anything, from purchase to imbibing.

I went off to Davidson College, while my best friends, Bill, David, and Doug, headed out to Florida State, King College, and Clemson University. We experienced our first semester not only away from home but away from each other for the first time since we had entered junior high school.

About a week after I got to Davidson, I was invited to go along on an outing to Charlotte on a Saturday night. We were going to go to a place called The Gondola and have pizza for dinner. This was going to be a big deal, since, as freshmen, we were not allowed to have cars. We had actually been included in a party put together by upperclassmen. My new friend Van Quinn was in charge of it all.

We drove into Charlotte and out on Morehead Street. I had never been to an Italian restaurant. In fact, I had never even tasted pizza other than a frozen one Mama had once had us try out when Daddy was gone to eat at the Lions Club on a Thursday night.

The Gondola was to me a magical place. There were little tables with red-checked tablecloths, and each of them had a wine bottle with a candle in it. The bottle was almost covered with wax drippings from all the candles it had held since the fall of Rome, and this seemed to me to be both artistic and romantic. We looked at the menu and, with Van's guidance, we ordered several different large pizzas that we could all share.

Then came the new world for me. Van looked up at the waiter like he did this every day of his life. "And we will have two large bottles of New York State Burgundy."

I did not even know that he was talking about wine until the bottles came and a funny-looking glass with a long stem between the top and bottom appeared beside my plate. The waiter had Van taste the wine, which he did and declared to be "acceptable," and then the waiter poured each of our funny glasses a little less than half full. I thought this to be strange and wondered why we were not getting a full glass.

Here is what I now remember. The first taste I had was not a sip but a gulp. I learned quickly that was not the way to drink wine. My shocked reaction to the gulp sent wine up the inside of my nose. I learned that one does not want wine up the inside of one's nose. Finally, I recovered and proceeded to take tiny sips, the taste mostly obscured by quick bites of pizza.

I must say that I slept very well that night and by the next day was convinced that I truly did know how to enjoy a glass of wine. During that entire first semester, I believe that I may have had a total of two, maybe three, small glasses of wine.

When the Christmas holidays came around, I was very anxious to get home to Waynesville and catch up with Bill, David, and Doug. We had tried to write to each other, but that did not really accomplish much. We needed some good time together to share stories, experiences, and all the new things we had separately learned in our first semester of higher education.

We got together almost the day we were home and had a great time laughing and telling about the stupid things we could admit to each other that we had tried to hide from our new college classmates, so they would not know how naive and inexperienced we were.

Then the discussion rolled around to alcohol. At that point, what we discovered was mutually amazing to us all. We discovered that each one of us—yes, all four of us—had, in one short semester, become consummate wine experts. We shared our vast experience with fine wines and talked about bouquet and taste and overtones with the best of them. I knew that I did not know what I was talking about, but the three of them sounded so knowledgeable that I had no idea they were as ignorant and inexperienced as I was. We were all working to impress.

By the time the evening was over, we had all decided that, before we went back to school, we had to get together and have ourselves a gourmet wine party.

The first problem was, where are we going to have it? None of our family homes would work. But Bill was at this time living with

My high-school graduation

his older half-sister, Sarah Ann, and she was working the night shift at the bowling-alley snack bar. So, each night, she left to go to work by about ten-thirty and did not get home until nearly seven-thirty the next morning. The location question was solved.

It was not unusual for us to spend the night with each other, so it was no big issue for each of us to announce that we were going to Asheville to a movie on Friday night and then were coming back to spend the night at Bill's house. (This actually sounded considerate, as it would keep each of us from waking our families as we returned home late.)

The next difficulty was buying the wine. We were all old enough, but everyone in Waynesville knew us and, at that time, Haywood County was still a dry county. We would have to do our shopping in Asheville.

On Friday afternoon, we met at Bill's house and checked to be sure that Sarah Ann knew about our plan and that she was indeed going to be out at work all night. Then we got into my mama's car (she had even offered it to the four of us) and headed for Asheville.

We went to supper at Buck's Restaurant on Tunnel Road and had such a good time that there was not enough time to locate a place to buy the wine before the movie started. So we headed on into town to the Imperial Theatre. I have no idea what movie we saw, as the rest of the night effectively erased many memories of the earlier evening. It was a seven o'clock movie, and when the film was over we started, about nine at night in Asheville, North Carolina, in the 1960s, to find a place still open that sold "fine wine."

We found one. It was on Merrimon Avenue and was called "7-Eleven." When we looked in the store, we discovered that it did indeed have a selection of very fine wines. They were modern wines, not the old-fashioned kind you had to pull cork out of but new wines that you had only to screw the top off. There were several kinds with names such as "Thunderbird" and "Wild Irish Rose." There was one kind, though, that really caught our attention. It was in round-shouldered bottles and had little woven baskets that actually were made right around the bottles themselves. It was called "Chianti," and it cost ten cents a bottle more than any other wine there.

Having the level of experience we all had, we did not know exactly how much we needed to buy. Then David solved the problem for us. "When my uncle Phil buys beer, he always gets a six-pack." So we bought six bottles of cheap 7-Eleven Chianti.

Our plan was originally to have wine and cheese, but the 7-Eleven did not have any cheese that night. So, instead, we got bread and butter. We all thought that would be just as good anyway. With our purchases all in hand, we paid the bill and headed back to Waynesville to begin the great wine party.

The remainder of the evening is still difficult for me to remember. It is like you took a lot of pictures on your vacation, but they all got dropped on the floor, and most of them blew away into the ocean. The ones that did not blow away were the ones you stepped on when you were trying to catch them, and these ones were marred and made difficult to see clearly because of the footprints.

One picture I remember is of sitting on a sofa that was upholstered in green plastic and watching two things at once. One eye was on Jack Paar on late-night black-and-white television, while the other eye was looking down the hall and watching Bill throwing up into the commode in the bathroom and thinking that it was the most normal scene in the world.

It was warm that night, and as the evening wore on it began to rain softly. I remember that we all walked out on the back porch of the house and stood there talking as the rain rolled off the porch roof behind us. David and I were standing with our backs to the wall, and Doug and Bill were standing with their backs to the edge of the porch. We had discovered that all four of us were taking different foreign languages our first year in college, so we were conversing brilliantly in all four of these one-semester new languages at the same time. It all made perfect sense.

As we talked, Bill leaned back a tiny bit, and seeing this from the corner of his eye, Doug leaned back to match him but went a bit farther. Bill leaned back more, then Doug, then Bill, then Doug, until all of a sudden both of them fell backwards off the porch. I remember that they both lay there on the ground, still speaking French and Spanish, as David and I leaned down over the edge of the porch and kept speaking German and Greek to them. And there was nothing that felt out of the ordinary about this at all.

Gradually, the rain tapered off into fog, and as morning began to creep toward us, we all somehow decided that it was too foggy for me to drive, so we would walk home, and I would come back and get Mama's car later. I can still remember being in the fog with no other traffic out at four in the morning, following the yellow line in the middle of the road all the way home—and hoping that I was following the correct yellow line. Once up our driveway, I slipped into the house very quietly, eased down the hall and into my bedroom, and fell into something that I thought to be sleep.

It lasted until well up into the following day. I awakened to discover that I had been sick in my sleep and was rolling in purple vomit that was completely covering the bedsheets and my pajamas. What to do now?

It was so late in the day that both Mama and Daddy were gone somewhere; both of their cars were absent from the driveway. So, in the protection of their absence, I gathered up the sheets and my pajamas and crammed them all into the washing machine at the same time. I added a large measure of Tide detergent, and when the agitation started, a huge mountain of purple soap bubbles began to come up out of the lid of the washing machine. In a near-panic, I picked up a glass gallon jug of Clorox and poured all that was left of it into the washing machine. When the cycle was all finished, the sheets and pajamas had almost totally disintegrated in the bottom of the washing machine. They were fit only for the trash. I made up the bed with new sheets and pillowcases and was sure that I had successfully gotten away with the entire happening.

The worst thing about the next two days was that I desperately needed to die but could not! I just stayed miserably and sickly alive. It was horrible. I did not call any of the other boys, and none of them called me; we all discovered later that we could not see the telephone clearly enough to see the numbers. And if we could have seen them, we still could not have gotten our fingers into the right holes in the dial. There have never been two more surpassingly miserable days in my entire life.

Gradually, I began to come out of the tunnel just a day or so before time to return to college. That night, we were having supper when Daddy looked over at me and said, "I haven't seen the boys much at all during this holiday vacation. It would be nice to see them before you go back to school. Why don't you call David and Bill and Doug and invite them over for supper tomorrow night? I'm sure your mama would make a big pot of spaghetti sauce, and we could just have a little time before we have to start missing all of you again." No excuses would be offered; the plan was set.

I managed to call all three of them. Nobody seemed to have very much to say. They were invited as Daddy had suggested, and the following evening all arrived at our house for the spaghetti supper as planned. We had a very nice and calm time. As I was eating spaghetti, I could not help thinking that somewhere in the world people were probably eating spaghetti and enjoyably drinking Chianti with it. It was a disgusting thought.

We finished our supper and kept visiting at the table. Mama, it turns out, had also made lemon meringue pie for our dessert. The pie was, as expected, quite wonderful. There were compliments all around.

I thought that things were about to wind down when all of a sudden Daddy spoke up to us. "Well, boys, we will miss all of you when you are gone. It may be a little while before we are all together again, so I thought I might tell you a little story."

I almost stopped breathing! There was nothing to do but listen.

Daddy started, "You know, I can't remember a time when my father, Donald's grandfather, was not running for political office of some kind. He held about every local office in Haywood County and was in the state legislature before I was born. Politics filled our household life.

"One day, I guess I was about twelve or thirteen years old, a man came out to our house to talk with Daddy about politics. It was probably a Sunday afternoon because neither one of them seemed to have anything to do, and they sat in the kitchen and drank coffee and talked about all afternoon.

"The interesting thing about this visit was that the man had arrived in a car. It was a Model T Ford, and it was in no way new. Even though the car was not new, it was one of the first cars we had ever seen, and maybe the first one we actually had a chance to touch. While Daddy and the man were talking in the kitchen on the back side of the house, we boys (that would have been Moody and Harry and Frank and me) went all over that car. We looked it all over, crawled under it, and looked at the bottom, and then actually climbed up on it and got in it. The convertible top was folded down, and getting in and out of the car was nothing at all. Frank sat in the driver's seat and made noises like he was driving the car.

"About that time, one of us saw a bottle sticking out from under the seat of the Model T. Frank or Harry, one, pulled the bottle out, and it turned out to be a bottle of homemade corn whiskey. It had a cork stuck in the top, and they pulled it out, and we all stood around and sniffed the bottle.

"We had a bunch of loose chickens that ran around on their own all over the place. They scratched up their own food and laid eggs here and there and were often volunteered for service as Sunday dinner. The chickens happened to be right there in the same part of the yard where we were sniffing the whiskey bottle. I don't know whose idea it was, but in a few minutes it was proposed that we try giving one of those chickens a drink of corn liquor.

"Frank caught a big hen and got her firmly under his arm. Then it was Harry who dribbled a little bit of corn liquor into the chicken's mouth as Frank held it open and Moody and I laughed. The chicken coughed and sputtered, but the corn liquor went down. They gave her a few more drinks, and then she got real wild and flopped and got loose from Frank and landed on the ground.

"Immediately, the chicken tried to run, but it fell over. It tried to get up, but it flopped around all over the ground. We were laughing our heads off, watching the chicken have a drunken fit in the yard, when Daddy and the man came out of the house, as their visit was over. Immediately, we got serious and as quiet as mice in church. We were all watching the chicken as Daddy also turned to look at it.

"The chicken kept flopping around, and when Daddy observed this he said, 'Boys, there's an old, sick chicken. One of you go and get a hoe or an ax and kill it. We don't want it to make the rest of our chickens sick. I've never seen a chicken act like that, so do it right now.'

"The four of us stood there. We knew that the chicken was not sick. We knew that it was a totally good chicken—good for laying eggs and good for eating, if we meant to kill it for supper. But we couldn't tell Daddy what had really happened or we would be in serious trouble. So Frank went around to the shed and got the ax, and we killed a perfectly good chicken."

Daddy paused like this was the end of the story. He slowly looked around the table at each of us and then looked away from us as he slowly said, "Yes, boys, if chickens drink too much, they're liable to get killed whether they deserve it or not."

And that was all that was ever said. Mama never had any idea why he told us that story. But we knew. The only thing we did not know was, once again, how he had managed to figure us out.

Two Birthdays

Daddy had two basic beliefs about travel: If you haven't been, then why do you need to go? If you have been, then why do you need to go back?

The consequence of these beliefs was that, in my childhood, our family never went anywhere. So I was thirty-seven years old before I ever applied for my first passport. I was not actually going anywhere at age thirty-seven. I simply discovered that I could get a passport for no reason, and then, if I ever got to go somewhere, I would be ready.

I went to the post office where my wife and I lived at that time in Lexington, North Carolina, and got all of the materials to apply for my first passport. I carefully read all the instructions, filled out the forms, gathered what was needed, and took it all back to the post office.

I was positively insulted that they would not accept the front page in my baby book as proof that I was born! It had my name and date of birth, it had the signature of one of the nurses at the hospital, it had my little baby footprint, and it even had my baby teeth, which had been fixed with yellowing Scotch tape around the edges of the page, where my mother had secured them after buying them back from the Tooth Fairy.

The instructions in the passport materials called for a birth certificate, and the postmaster insisted the baby book was not a proper birth certificate. I was told that I had to go back to Waynesville—back to Haywood County, where I was born—go to the courthouse to the register of deeds office, and there get a certified and sealed copy of my *real* birth certificate. And so the plan was made.

Several weeks later, when I set aside time for the little trip, I headed out to Waynesville and arrived at my parents' house, my childhood home, and told them what I was doing. After Daddy growled about how nobody needed a passport anyway, I shared dinner and spent the night with them, then headed the next day up to the Haywood County Courthouse to obtain proof that I was born. I found a parking place right on Main Street and walked up the long sidewalk to the courthouse. I knew who was going to be in the register of deeds office long before I even entered the main courthouse door. It would be J. B. Siler, who had been the register of deeds when Adam named the animals in the early days of the creation. He had been there forever and knew everything that it was legal to know about everyone who ever lived anytime at all in Haywood County.

When I entered the office, sure enough, J. B. was there. He knew me on sight. I had grown up with and gone to school with his children. Mr. Siler spoke politely, then asked me what I needed that he could help with.

"I have come to get a copy of my birth certificate," I said. "I am applying for a passport, and I need positive proof that I was born."

After I had to give embarrassingly empty answers about the trip I was surely planning, he got ready to go into the back of the office and look for the birth certificate. Mr. Siler asked, "When were you born? That's the way they are all filed, so if I know that, it is a lot easier to find it."

I always loved my birthday. It came on the first day of June, and in those days that was about when school got out for the summer. For many years, I was convinced that school got out for the summer because it was my birthday; it was my own special birthday present.

I answered, "I was born on the first day of June in 1944."

He nodded and disappeared from behind the counter back into the depths of file cabinets.

In a few minutes, he returned. "I can't find it where it ought to be," he frowned. "Maybe I didn't understand you. Tell me again when you were born."

"June the first, 1944," I repeated.

"Let me have another try. It was at the Haywood County Hospital?"

I nodded, and he disappeared.

This time, he was gone for a long time. When he came back, he was laughing as he laid an official-looking document on the countertop between us. "Here it is. You better take a look at it."

I picked up the birth certificate. It was mine, all right; it had my name on it. And it was correct in every way except it said that in 1944 I was born on the ninth day of July.

I paid the required fifty cents for a sealed copy and headed back out to my parents' house in a determined hurry. I needed to learn the story of how I came to have two birthdays, one of which I had never heard of.

When I got to the top of the driveway, my mama's car was missing. *Oh, good,* I thought. *Maybe I will have Daddy all to myself, and there will be a better chance of finding out the truth, and the story will be a good one.*

When I walked in the door, Daddy told me that Mama had gone to the Ladye Faire Beauty Parlor. That usually took about two semesters, and so I knew we were going to be uninterrupted for the entire afternoon.

In our yard, when I was six or seven

That afternoon, when I was thirty-seven years old and Daddy was eighty-two, I heard for the first and only time in my life my father's entire story of the day on which I was born. I think back now to how easily I could have missed the entire thing.

He looked at the birth certificate copy I handed him and then looked back at me like he was not surprised at all. "I guess this is what you want to know about," he asserted.

"I guess you are right!" I smiled at him, and he started.

"You already know that your mother and I did not get married when I was a young man. I was past forty before I ever met her for the first time."

I knew this part of the story but said nothing as he repeated all of it to me in his own time.

"I never actually thought that I would get married, after spending all those years being sure that Frank and Mary and Esther and Lee and Ruth got grown up after my father died in 1920. I was nineteen when he died, and the little children didn't have anybody but Mama and Aunt Laura to take care of them. Besides,

I had to take care of those two old ladies also. They needed more help than the children did.

"So, when I married your mama, it was a big surprise to a lot of people—most of all a big surprise to me! Then, when it looked like a baby was coming along, nobody could believe it at all. This was going to be a real miracle."

I listened patiently, as I knew somehow that he was telling me a story that was not practiced in any way.

He told me that the plan was for the baby to be born in the hospital, and that it would be the first time a baby in the family had ever been born in a hospital, and everyone was a little bit uncertain about that.

"Well," he went on, "it was early in the morning when your mama woke me up and told me she thought it was time for her to go to the hospital. She was having pains, and she was not sure when she was supposed to go, so she thought we had better go on.

"I told her to get up and get dressed and then to walk around in a circle in the kitchen. And while she was doing that, I would go milk Helen, our Guernsey milk cow. The cow had to be milked even if a baby was coming.

"As soon as I got back to the house, we got her little suitcase and got in the car to go to the hospital. As we backed out of the driveway, I looked over at the garden on the opposite side of the driveway. It was the first day of June, and I had the best little knee-high stand of corn you had ever seen that early in the year. You know that I was always in 'garden wars' with all of the in-laws. Every spring, I would start planting stuff when I knew it was way too early. Some of it would always get frozen, but once in a while something would slip through and I would be way ahead of all the brothers-in-law. They never could figure out how I did it.

"So, this year, there had been no late freeze, and there on the first day of June I had a pretty little stand of Golden Cross Bantam sweet corn that was nearly knee high. You couldn't keep from looking over there and admiring it even on the way to the hospital when the baby was coming."

I was suddenly aware that he was telling a story about "the

baby" without referring to the coming child as me. There was something already emerging as a little bit scary about this whole narrative.

Daddy went on. "We got to the hospital—you know, the old hospital out in East Waynesville—and I took your mama inside and got her checked in. They took her on in the back and told me to go and sit in a little room off to the side on the first floor. The nurses told me that they would come and get me when there was anything that I needed to know. In 1944, that was as close to the delivery room as fathers were allowed to go. I went into the little room and sat there wishing that I had thought to at least bring a book to read while I was waiting. Never having done this before, I had no idea how long it was going to be or what was coming next."

As he told me the next part of the story, I knew he was blending his own experience and memory with what he later learned from Mama, as he was not directly with her when much of it happened.

He told me that the nurses in the delivery room called for the doctor to come. The doctor did not come. They called him a second time, and still he did not come. When they called him the third time and he did not come, they decided that they were bothering him, and they did not call again, figuring that he would arrive when he thought it was right.

Sometime around two in the afternoon, the doctor arrived. He examined my mother and said to her, "You should have had a Cesarean, but it is too late!" like it was somehow her fault. He then turned and walked out of the delivery room.

Daddy told me that he had been sitting there in the little room for about eight hours when suddenly the door opened and the doctor walked in. Daddy jumped up and approached the doctor to get the news and was met with an unexpected question from the doctor: "Which one do you want, your baby or your wife?"

At this moment, I heard the sniffling sound and looked at Daddy's face to see the tears streaming down as he told me the story.

He went on, "Son, I didn't even know you! I never ever thought that I would get married to begin with, and I knew that I would never get married again. So I looked at the doctor and told him, 'I have to have my wife!' "

The doctor turned and left the room.

Later on, Daddy learned from my mother that she endured a horrible forceps delivery that left her in terrible shape and with a baby that was so battered and bruised that they would not let her see her baby for three days. She was convinced that the baby had died and that they simply did not want to tell her.

No one thought to go out and tell my father anything. He was left to sit there alone for the entire afternoon.

Sometime late in the afternoon, the door opened and a nurse entered the waiting room where he had spent the day. Eager for news, he stood up at her entrance.

"Well, they're both alive for now, but don't expect anything." Then she told him, "We need a name. Have you thought of a name for the baby?"

My father's name is Joe. My grandfather's name is Joe. My younger brother's name is Joe. I had always wondered why my younger brother got this name instead of its landing on me.

Then Daddy told me, "They said you were probably going to die, so I just made up a name."

That is when I understood why there was no one named either Donald or Douglas on either side of the family.

Suddenly, Daddy's story picked up speed. "It was the end of the day. I had been there imprisoned in that little room for twelve hours. There had been not more than a minute of total conversation that day, both thirty-second versions of which had been awful. For some reason, I looked at my watch. It was exactly six o'clock. The cow had to be milked!"

He went on to tell me that he didn't even think about calling anyone else because the need to milk the cow gave him a brief reason to leave the hospital. And after this day, if he couldn't get out of there for a few minutes, he was going to die. So he ran out the hospital door and down the steps to his black Plymouth. He jumped in the car and headed out of town to Plott Creek Road.

Just as Daddy swung the Plymouth into our driveway, his eyes wandered over to his garden. There stood Helen, our cow. She had pushed her way out of the pasture fence and was standing there in the garden, very happily munching away on Daddy's new stand of corn.

He braked the car to a quick stop and jumped out. Then he broke what he called "a two-handed limb" off a big maple tree in the yard and chased after the old cow. She saw him coming and ran right back through the hole she had made in the pasture fence to begin with.

Following her into the pasture, Daddy started whipping the cow with the maple limb. She ran, and he chased and whipped her. She was bellowing, and he was whipping with all his might.

"All of a sudden"—he was looking at me with clear eyes now— "that old cow stopped running and looked me straight in the eyes. She said, *Mmoooooooo!* and I understood exactly what she was saying. She was saying to me, 'Joe Davis, you are not whipping a cow for eating your corn. You are just using me to try to beat the daylights out of everything that has happened this day.' "

He told me that he then hugged the old cow around the neck and started petting and scratching her on the back of her head. She bellowed and he bellowed, she cried and he cried, she licked him and he didn't tell me whether he licked her! They just stood there together until Daddy had cried out all of the tears that were in him.

Then he walked over to the feed room at the barn and got her a big bucket of dairy mash. He got his milk bucket and milked that dear old cow while she enjoyed the extra-sized helping of dairy mash. After she was milked, he led her out of the pasture and back into the garden, where he petted her while he let her eat every bit of that new, fresh corn right down to the ground.

The end of the story was coming now. "You know, son, after I retired from the bank, I had a job in the magistrate's office at the post office. J. B. Siler and I were always hanging around together because people coming to the magistrate's office to get married had to get their license from him first. One thing I learned about recordkeeping is that you are supposed to file a certificate of live birth within twenty-four hours.

"Here's what I think happened. I don't think that doctor actually realized that he was going to have a live birth with you, so he forgot to do it. Sometime, maybe about six weeks later, he must have been cleaning up his desk and came onto some paperwork he had not finished. So, to keep him from getting in trouble, it looks like you then got born on the ninth of July."

And that was it.

So I have two birthdays. One of them is the first day of June, the way it has always been. The other is not the ninth of July. No, my other birthday is the wonderful day when my father told me that story. I was thirty-seven years old with three sons, and I had spent my entire life thinking that fathers feel no pain in childbirth. I cannot imagine the pain my own father endured in the course of that long day.

I only wish I had somehow known how to ask for the story sooner. If I had, I might have been able to save both of us a lot of the voluntary pain I was good at producing later, especially during my teenage years. And I might have come to know much sooner how very precious, no matter how it comes to us, is every tiny moment of human life.